12 Steps Study Success

Conrad Lashley and Warwick Best

continuum
LONDON • NEW YORK

Also available from Continuum:

Thinking Visually: Craig
Career Skills: Forsyth
Informative Writing (Second Edition): Goddard
Passing Exams: Hamilton
How to Get into Advertising: Neidle
Dissertation Skills for Business and Management Students: White

Continuum
The Tower Building   370 Lexington Avenue
11 York Road   New York
London SE1 7NX   NY 10017-6503

www.continuumbooks.com

First published in 2001
This edition published in 2003

British Library Cataloguing-in-Publication Data
A catalogue record for this book is available from the British Library.

ISBN 0-8264-6790-3

Designed and typeset by Ben Cracknell Studios
Printed and bound in Great Britain

Contents

Part C **Study competence**

PART A

Guide to the Study Skills Text

Introduction

This book gives you suggestions about how to improve your approach to study and learning. It will help in developing the skills you will need for effective use of your time and for the successful completion of assessed activities.

Although the book is primarily designed for students newly enrolled on courses at colleges and universities, *the ideas apply to anyone*, from those just starting a course to people returning to study after a break. The suggestions for effective study can be used in every type of learning situation:

✦ at college or university

✦ at work

✦ in adult education

✦ for pleasure and leisure

The materials have been used in courses at Nottingham Business School and also the School of Tourism and Hospitality Management at Leeds Metropolitan University for some years. They have provided the basis for the development of student learning and have resulted in impressive improvements in student outputs and performance.

12 Steps to Study Success makes three core assumptions about study, learning and performance.

Firstly, it is assumed that successful learning and assessment are related to the use of systematic study techniques, which are rarely addressed in formal education. Most courses tell people what to study and not how to study.

> **Most people can learn to be more effective in the way they study and approach assessment.**

The **second** assumption, which will be outlined more fully later, is that active involvement is an essential component of learning.

> **You will gain most by completing the exercises and activities contained in the book.**

Finally, it is assumed that effective study and assessment will be a product of competent performance. Performance criteria define competent performance and provide a standard against which to measure your own performance.

> **An ongoing commitment to improve the standard of your work will stem from the use of performance criteria.**

The Structure of the Book

The book is presented in three parts. **Part A** provides an introduction and makes some suggestions as to how you might use the book most effectively.

Part B contains the twelve Study Steps, which give you advice, guidance and information about how best to organize study and approach assessed activities. Whilst each of these steps or chapters covers different material, they are not written in such a way that they need to be read sequentially, with each step dependent on the previous one. It is hoped that the reader will cover all the steps, but it is quite acceptable to dip into sections independently.

Each Study Step starts with an outline of the issues to be covered and finishes with a summary of the key points raised. The sessions follow *three broad themes*. **The first** deals with issues relevant to an *understanding of the learning process* and the different styles and strategies which students adopt. **The second** provides guidance for *improving study techniques* through effective time management, reading, note-taking, behaviour in lectures, and how best to gather and present information. **The third** theme aims to *develop your understanding of what lecturers will expect from you in assessed activities*. Thus, if you are writing a report or an essay, or making a presentation, use the relevant Study Sessions as the basis for your preparation.

Part C defines performance criteria associated with each Study Session. There are a number of ways you can use these, but they are designed to enable you to demonstrate competent performance.

How to Use this Book

Effective improvement in approaches to the various study tasks is individual and personal. *You* are best placed to monitor your own performance and its development. Self-study techniques are the key approach. You are advised to work through each Study Session, completing the various activities as appropriate.

Having worked through a Study Session in Part B, turn to the relevant competence sheet in Part C and attempt to demonstrate competence by applying the performance criteria. Where necessary, produce the evidence of competence.

There are a number of ways you can work through the text.

Working on your own

It is possible to work through these exercises on your own. The key here is *to be rigorously critical* of the *evidence* which you *produce*. Feedback from performance is also helpful. Each activity which you undertake should be subject to critical self-evaluation, whether it be

12 STEPS TO STUDY SUCCESS

→ understanding learning styles

→ organizing study

→ managing your time

→ reading

→ making notes

→ attending lectures or tutorials

→ gathering information

→ presenting numerical data

→ writing essays and reports

→ making presentations

→ sitting examinations

→ writing your dissertation

Use the Learning Cycle outlined in Step 1 (Figure 1.3) as a way of self-evaluation.

Having undergone the activity, think about what it felt like. What went well and what went not so well? What do you need to improve on for next time? What will you do next time?

The process of undertaking an activity and considering what it felt like, followed by a period to reflect upon your performance and think about what you need to do next time, is fundamental to improving your performance.

Working in pairs or small groups

Whilst learning and studying are personal and individual activities, the judgement and approaches taken by other students can be helpful in the learning process. Remember, you are learning to shape your own expectations of your performance. The ability to be self-critical against a professional standard is the key to success on most courses and in work situations. Other people's expectations and views, together with subsequent feedback from performance, are crucial aids to learning.

→ Working with another person, or in a small group of three or four, complete the competence sheet in Part C.

→ Switch round the evidence sheets so that you assess another person's efforts and someone else assesses yours.

Has the person demonstrated that they have understood the principles outlined in the Study Session?
Has the person provided sufficient evidence that they are now competent in that study skill?
Has the person provided evidence to support the various performance criteria?

Once you are satisfied that the person has met the criteria and demonstrated competence in the study skill, sign them off by initialling the sheet in the box provided.

If a person does not demonstrate competence after the first attempt, let them go away and rework the exercise, or produce additional evidence later. Each individual needs to consider the steps outlined above. Keep repeating the process until the required performance criteria have been met.

Remember, this approach is based on achieving a competent standard; it is not just about working through the text. It is likely that effective performance will only be achieved when a person is competent. Competence is defined as demonstrating the relevant performance criteria.

Developing study skills through the course

In some cases the course on which you are studying may use this text as the basis for planning and coordinating the development of student learning. This is an approach developed at Nottingham Business School and also the School of Tourism and Hospitality Management at Leeds Metropolitan University.

The course team makes student learning the centrepiece of course planning. Teaching, learning and assessment strategies are based on a model of experiential learning.

Each student then works through *12 Steps to Study Success* and produces a portfolio of study competence. The personal tutor guides students through the process and advises them on study skills development.

All assessed work is graded and marked against the assessment criteria given for reports, essays and presentations.

Students are encouraged to reflect upon their performance and consider how they can correct faults and build on strengths in their work.

Study Skills Audit

Before you work through the Study Sessions, complete the study skills audit below. Try to be as accurate as possible. For each statement, circle the number that corresponds most closely to your study techniques.

Study Skills Audit	never	seldom	occasionally	sometimes	always
I use a wide range of learning styles.	1	2	3	4	5
I apply learning-style theory to my study.	1	2	3	4	5
I use memory aids to assist in learning.	1	2	3	4	5
I use time-management techniques.	1	2	3	4	5
I design and use a study timetable.	1	2	3	4	5
I use a range of reading techniques during study.	1	2	3	4	5
I use keyword noting techniques.	1	2	3	4	5
I use numerical data to support my reports.	1	2	3	4	5
I use different learning techniques in lectures, seminars and tutorials.	1	2	3	4	5

	never	seldom	occasionally	sometimes	always
I use formal referencing systems when writing essays.	1	2	3	4	5
I have a professional approach to making verbal presentations.	1	2	3	4	5
I prepare fully for examinations.	1	2	3	4	5
I use a range of research methods when undertaking primary research.	1	2	3	4	5
I use a range of information-retrieval techniques when studying.	1	2	3	4	5

Total your score and compare it with the key over the page.

TOTAL

KEY TO SCORES

15 to 29

There are many aspects of your study skill competence which are in urgent need of further development. Work through all the sessions and complete all sections of Part C.

30 to 59

Examine the profile of your scores and adopt the appropriate study strategy. It may be that you need to work through all the sessions because your scores reveal general problems in all areas. On the other hand it may be that particular sessions need to be targeted. Work through all sections of Part C.

60 to 75

There may well be room for improvement in some key areas. Are you sure that you are not being overconfident? Focus on those sessions where you register weakness. Work through all sections of Part C.

PART B

Study Steps

Learning Styles

In this step you will consider:

✓ *Your preferred learning style*

✓ *The benefits of this and other learning styles*

✓ *How to learn more effectively by adopting a style which takes account of experiential learning*

Introduction

Most people have a preferred learning style – in other words, ways of going about learning which has developed over years in school or college. As one of education's successes you may feel that this approach has served you well in the past and you might as well carry on as before.

This session aims to provide you with an introduction to a number of theories of learning styles. This will enable you to understand your own approach better and adapt your style to be most effective during your time as a student.

How to Go About It

The first step is to identify your own learning style preferences.

Learning styles questionnaire

This questionnaire (Table 1.1) is designed to find your preferred learning style(s). Over the years you have developed learning 'habits' that help you benefit more from some experiences than from others. Since you are probably unaware of this, the questionnaire will help you pinpoint your learning preferences so that you are in a better position to select learning strategies that suit your style.

Complete the questionnaire, trying to be as honest as you can. There is no time limit, but it will probably take you 20 to 25 minutes. The accuracy of the results depends on how honest you are. There are no right or wrong answers. Please mark each item with a tick in the relevant box.

Table 1.1 Learning Styles Questionnaire

Statement	SD strongly disagree	D disagree	DoB disagree on balance	AoB agree on balance	A agree	SA strongly agree
	0	1	2	3	4	5
1. I have strong beliefs about what is right and wrong, good and bad.	☐	☐	☐	☐	☐	☐
2. I often 'throw caution to the wind'.	☐	☐	☐	☐	☐	☐
3. I tend to solve problems using a step-by-step approach, avoiding any 'flights of fancy'.	☐	☐	☐	☐	☐	☐
4. I believe that formal procedures and policies cramp people's style.	☐	☐	☐	☐	☐	☐
5. I have a reputation for having a no-nonsense, 'call a spade a spade' style.	☐	☐	☐	☐	☐	☐
6. I often find that actions based on 'gut feelings' are as sound as those based on careful thought and analysis.	☐	☐	☐	☐	☐	☐
7. I like to do the sort of work where I have time to 'leave no stone unturned'.	☐	☐	☐	☐	☐	☐
8. I regularly question people about their basic assumptions.	☐	☐	☐	☐	☐	☐
9. What matters most is whether something works in practice.	☐	☐	☐	☐	☐	☐
10. I actively seek out new experiences.	☐	☐	☐	☐	☐	☐

11. When I hear about a new idea or approach I immediately start working out how to apply it in practice.	☐	☐	☐	☐	☐	☐
12. I am keen on self-discipline, such as watching my diet, taking regular exercise, sticking to a fixed routine, etc.	☐	☐	☐	☐	☐	☐
13. I take pride in doing a thorough job.	☐	☐	☐	☐	☐	☐
14. I get on best with logical, analytical people and less well with spontaneous, 'irrational' people.	☐	☐	☐	☐	☐	☐
15. I take care over the interpretation of data available to me and avoid jumping to conclusions.	☐	☐	☐	☐	☐	☐
16. I like to reach a decision carefully after weighing up many alternatives.	☐	☐	☐	☐	☐	☐
17. I'm attracted more to novel, unusual ideas than to practical ones.	☐	☐	☐	☐	☐	☐
18. I don't like 'loose ends' and prefer to fit things into a coherent pattern.	☐	☐	☐	☐	☐	☐
19. I accept and stick to laid-down procedures and policies so long as I regard them as an efficient way of getting the job done.	☐	☐	☐	☐	☐	☐
20. I like to relate my actions to a general principle.	☐	☐	☐	☐	☐	☐
21. In discussions I like to get straight to the point.	☐	☐	☐	☐	☐	☐

22. I tend to have distant, rather formal relationships with people at work.

☐ ☐ ☐ ☐ ☐ ☐

23. I thrive on the challenge of tackling something new and different.

☐ ☐ ☐ ☐ ☐ ☐

24. I enjoy fun-loving, spontaneous people.

☐ ☐ ☐ ☐ ☐ ☐

25. I pay meticulous attention to detail before coming to a conclusion.

☐ ☐ ☐ ☐ ☐ ☐

26. I find it difficult to come up with wild, off-the-top-of-the-head ideas.

☐ ☐ ☐ ☐ ☐ ☐

27. I don't believe in wasting time by 'beating around the bush'.

☐ ☐ ☐ ☐ ☐ ☐

28. I am careful not to jump to conclusions too quickly.

☐ ☐ ☐ ☐ ☐ ☐

29. I prefer to have as many sources of information as possible – the more data to mull over, the better.

☐ ☐ ☐ ☐ ☐ ☐

30. Flippant people who don't take things seriously enough usually irritate me.

☐ ☐ ☐ ☐ ☐ ☐

31. I listen to other people's point of view before putting forward my own.

☐ ☐ ☐ ☐ ☐ ☐

32. I tend to be open about how I'm feeling.

☐ ☐ ☐ ☐ ☐ ☐

33. In discussions I enjoy watching the manoeuvring of the other participants.

☐ ☐ ☐ ☐ ☐ ☐

34. I prefer to respond to events on a spontaneous, flexible basis, rather than plan things out in advance.

☐ ☐ ☐ ☐ ☐ ☐

12 STEPS TO STUDY SUCCESS

35. I tend to be attracted to techniques such as network analysis, flow charts, branching programmes, contingency planning, etc.

☐ ☐ ☐ ☐ ☐ ☐

36. It worries me if I have to rush out a piece of work to meet a tight deadline.

☐ ☐ ☐ ☐ ☐ ☐

37. I tend to judge people's ideas on their practical merits.

☐ ☐ ☐ ☐ ☐ ☐

38. Quiet, thoughtful people tend to make me feel uneasy.

☐ ☐ ☐ ☐ ☐ ☐

39. I often get irritated by people who want to rush headlong into things.

☐ ☐ ☐ ☐ ☐ ☐

40. It is more important to enjoy the present moment than to think about the past or future.

☐ ☐ ☐ ☐ ☐ ☐

41. I think that decisions based on a thorough analysis of all the information are sounder than those based on intuition.

☐ ☐ ☐ ☐ ☐ ☐

42. I tend to be a perfectionist.

☐ ☐ ☐ ☐ ☐ ☐

43. In discussions I usually pitch in with lots of off-the-top-of-the-head ideas.

☐ ☐ ☐ ☐ ☐ ☐

44. In meetings I put forward practical, realistic ideas.

☐ ☐ ☐ ☐ ☐ ☐

45. More often than not, rules are there to be broken.

☐ ☐ ☐ ☐ ☐ ☐

46. I prefer to stand back from a situation and consider all the perspectives.

☐ ☐ ☐ ☐ ☐ ☐

47. I can often see inconsistencies and weaknesses in other people's arguments.

☐ ☐ ☐ ☐ ☐ ☐

48. On balance I talk more than I listen.

☐ ☐ ☐ ☐ ☐ ☐

49. I can often see better, more practical ways to get things done.

☐ ☐ ☐ ☐ ☐ ☐

50. I think written reports should be short, punchy and to the point.

☐ ☐ ☐ ☐ ☐ ☐

51. I believe that rational, logical thinking should win the day.

☐ ☐ ☐ ☐ ☐ ☐

52. I tend to discuss specific things with people rather than engaging in 'small talk'.

☐ ☐ ☐ ☐ ☐ ☐

53. I like people who have both feet firmly on the ground.

☐ ☐ ☐ ☐ ☐ ☐

54. In discussions I get impatient with irrelevancies and 'red herrings'.

☐ ☐ ☐ ☐ ☐ ☐

55. If I have a report to write I tend to produce lots of drafts before settling on the final version.

☐ ☐ ☐ ☐ ☐ ☐

56. I am keen to try things out to see if they work in practice.

☐ ☐ ☐ ☐ ☐ ☐

57. I am keen to reach answers via a logical approach.

☐ ☐ ☐ ☐ ☐ ☐

58. I enjoy being the one that talks a lot.

☐ ☐ ☐ ☐ ☐ ☐

59. In discussions I often find that I am the realist, keeping people to the point and avoiding 'cloud nine' speculations. ☐ ☐ ☐ ☐ ☐ ☐

60. I like to ponder many alternatives before making up my mind. ☐ ☐ ☐ ☐ ☐ ☐

61. In discussions with people I often find I am the most dispassionate and objective. ☐ ☐ ☐ ☐ ☐ ☐

62. In discussions I'm more likely to adopt a 'low profile' than to take the lead and do most of the talking. ☐ ☐ ☐ ☐ ☐ ☐

63. I like to be able to relate current actions to a long-term bigger picture. ☐ ☐ ☐ ☐ ☐ ☐

64. When things go wrong I am happy to shrug it off and 'put it down to experience'. ☐ ☐ ☐ ☐ ☐ ☐

65. I tend to reject wild, off-the-top-of-the-head ideas as being impractical. ☐ ☐ ☐ ☐ ☐ ☐

66. It's best to 'look before you leap'. ☐ ☐ ☐ ☐ ☐ ☐

67. On balance I do the listening rather than the talking. ☐ ☐ ☐ ☐ ☐ ☐

68. I tend to be tough on people who find it difficult to adopt a logical approach. ☐ ☐ ☐ ☐ ☐ ☐

69. Most times I believe the end justifies the means. ☐ ☐ ☐ ☐ ☐ ☐

70. I don't mind hurting other people's feelings so long as the job gets done.

☐ ☐ ☐ ☐ ☐ ☐

71. I find the formality of having specific objectives and plans stifling.

☐ ☐ ☐ ☐ ☐ ☐

72. I'm usually the 'life and soul' of the party.

☐ ☐ ☐ ☐ ☐ ☐

73. I do whatever is expedient to get the job done.

☐ ☐ ☐ ☐ ☐ ☐

74. I quickly get bored with methodical, detailed work.

☐ ☐ ☐ ☐ ☐ ☐

75. I am keen on exploring the basic assumptions, principles and theories underpinning things and events.

☐ ☐ ☐ ☐ ☐ ☐

76. I'm always interested to find out what other people think.

☐ ☐ ☐ ☐ ☐ ☐

77. I like meetings to be run on methodical lines, sticking to a laid-down agenda.

☐ ☐ ☐ ☐ ☐ ☐

78. I steer clear of subjective or ambiguous topics.

☐ ☐ ☐ ☐ ☐ ☐

79. I enjoy the drama and excitement of a crisis situation.

☐ ☐ ☐ ☐ ☐ ☐

80. People often find me insensitive to their feelings.

☐ ☐ ☐ ☐ ☐ ☐

Scoring the learning styles questionnaire

Enter your results on the scoring sheet given in Table 1.2 (opposite).

Table 1.2 Learning Styles Score Sheet

Question	Your Score	Question	Your Score	Question	Your Score	Question	Your Score
2	___	7	___	1	___	5	___
4	___	13	___	3	___	9	___
6	___	15	___	8	___	11	___
10	___	16	___	12	___	19	___
17	___	25	___	14	___	21	___
23	___	28	___	18	___	27	___
24	___	29	___	20	___	35	___
32	___	31	___	22	___	37	___
34	___	33	___	26	___	44	___
38	___	36	___	30	___	49	___
40	___	39	___	42	___	50	___
43	___	41	___	47	___	53	___
45	___	46	___	51	___	54	___
48	___	52	___	57	___	56	___
58	___	55	___	61	___	59	___
64	___	60	___	63	___	65	___
71	___	62	___	68	___	69	___
72	___	66	___	75	___	70	___
74	___	67	___	77	___	73	___
79	___	76	___	78	___	80	___
Totals							
	___		___		___		___
	Activist		Reflector		Theorist		Pragmatist

Total your score of points in each of the four columns. You should now have a score against four styles of learning: Activist; Reflector; Theorist; Pragmatist. Check the strength of your preference for each style by using the checklist in Table 1.3. The following pages describe each style in detail. You should be able to identify your own preferences from this. Typically, you may have a very strong preference for one style, but you may find that you have preferences for more than one style. As we shall see in a moment, this is healthy and reflects a rounded approach to study and learning.

This model is based on the work of Honey and Mumford and you should read their *Using Your Learning Styles* (London, BBC Books, 1995) for more detailed information. Essentially their view is that students need to identify the style(s) which they most prefer and then arrange learning experiences which match their preferences.

In other words, activists learn through active experiences; reflectors learn through observation; theorists learn through intellectual analysis; and pragmatists learn through examples of practical experiences.

Activists involve themselves fully and without bias in new experiences. They enjoy the 'here and now' and are happy to be dominated by immediate experiences. They are open-minded, not sceptical, and this tends to make them enthusiastic about anything new. Their philosophy is 'I'll try anything once'. They tend to act first and consider the consequences afterwards. Their days are filled with activity. They tackle problems by brainstorming. As soon as the excitement from one activity has died down they are busy looking for the next. They tend to thrive on the challenge of new experiences but are bored with implementation and longer-term consolidation. They are gregarious people, constantly involving themselves with others, but in doing so they seek to centre all activities around themselves.

Table 1.3 Learning Styles Profile Based on General Norms

ACTIVIST	REFLECTOR	THEORIST	PRAGMATIST	
100	100	100	100	
95	95	95	95	
90	90	90	90	
85		85	85	Very strong preference
80		80		
75				
70				
65				
60	85	75	80	
	80			Strong preference
55	75	70	75	
50	70	65	70	
45	65	60	65	Moderate preference
40	60	55	60	
35				
30	55	50	55	
25	50	45	50	Low Preference
20	45	40	45	
			40	
	35	35	35	
	30	30	30	
	25	25	25	
	20	20	20	Very low preference
15	15	15	15	
10	10	10	10	
5	5	5	5	
0	0	0	0	

Source: Adapted from P. Honey and A. Mumford, *Using Your Learning Styles* (London: BBC Books, 1995).

Activists learn best from activities where:

◆ There are new experiences/problems/opportunities from which to learn.

◆ They can engross themselves in short 'here and now' activities such as business games, competitive teamwork tasks and role-playing exercises.

◆ They have a lot of the limelight, they lead discussions, give presentations.

◆ They are allowed to generate ideas without restrictions of policy.

◆ They are thrown in at the deep end with a task they think difficult.

◆ They are involved with other people; solving problems as a team.

◆ It is appropriate to 'have a go'.

Reflectors like to stand back to ponder experiences and observe them from different perspectives. They collect data, both first hand and from others, and prefer to think about it thoroughly before coming to any conclusion. Because the thorough collection and analysis of data about experiences and events is what counts, they tend to postpone reaching definitive conclusions for as long as possible. Their philosophy is to be cautious. They are thoughtful people who like to consider all possible angles and implications before making a move. They enjoy observing other people in action. They listen to others and get the drift of the discussion before making their own points. They tend to adopt a low profile and have a slightly distant, tolerant, unruffled air about them. When they act it is part of a wide picture which includes the past as well as the present and others' observations as well as their own.

Reflectors learn best from activities where:

◆ They are allowed to watch/think/chew over activities.

◆ They are able to stand back and observe; observing a group at work, watch films/videos, etc.

◆ They are allowed to think before acting and have time to prepare.

◆ They can carry out painstaking research, investigation and probing.

◆ They have time to review what has happened, what they have learnt.

◆ They are required to produce carefully considered analyses and reports.

◆ They are helped to exchange views within a structured learning experience.

◆ They can reach a decision without pressure within their own time.

Theorists adapt and integrate observations into complex but logically sound theories. They think problems through in a vertical, step-by-step, logical way. They assimilate disparate facts into coherent theories. They tend to be perfectionists who won't rest easy until things are tidy and fit into a rational scheme. They like to analyse and synthesize. They are keen on basic assumptions, principles, theories, models and systems thinking. Their philosophy prizes rationality and logic: 'If it's logical it's good.' Questions they frequently ask are: 'Does it make sense?' 'How does it fit with that?' 'What are the basic assumptions?' They tend to be detached, analytical and dedicated to rational objectivity rather than anything subjective or ambiguous. Their approach to problems is consistently logical. This is their 'mental set'. They rigidly reject anything that doesn't fit with it. They prefer to maximize certainty and feel uncomfortable with subjective judgements, lateral thinking and flippant remarks.

Theorists learn best from activities where:

◆ The learning material is part of a system, model, concept or theory.

◆ They have time to explore the associations and relationships between ideas, events and situations.

◆ They have the chance to question and probe the basic methodology, assumptions and logic behind something.

◆ They are intellectually stretched, i.e. analysing a complex problem, being tested in a tutorial session, being asked searching questions.

◆ They are in structured situations with a clear purpose.

◆ They can read or listen to ideas and concepts that are rational and logical.

◆ They can analyse and then generalize problems.

◆ They are offered interesting ideas and concepts even if they are not relevant.

Pragmatists are keen on trying out ideas, theories and techniques to see if they work in practice. They positively search out new ideas and take the first opportunity to experiment with applications. They are the sort of people who return from courses brimming with new ideas that they want to try out in practice. They like to get on with things and act quickly and confidently on ideas that attract them.

12 STEPS TO STUDY SUCCESS

They tend to be impatient with ruminating and open-ended discussions. They are essentially practical, down-to-earth people who like making practical decisions and solving problems. They respond to problems and opportunities 'as a challenge'. Their philosophy is: 'There is always a better way' and 'If it works it's good'.

Pragmatists learn best from activities where:

◆ There is an obvious link between the subject and a practical problem.

◆ They are shown techniques that have obvious practical advantages.

◆ They have the chance to try out and practise techniques with an expert who can provide feedback.

◆ They are shown a model they can copy, a successful person, a film showing how something is done, etc.

◆ They are given immediate opportunities to try out what they have learnt.

◆ They are given good simulations and real problems to solve.

◆ They can concentrate on practical situations.

Look at Table 1.4 and compare the advantages of your preferred style with those of the other styles. When you have done this, look at the disadvantages of each style given in Table 1.5.

Table 1.4 Advantages of Each Learning Style

Activist	*Reflector*
You:	You:
✦ get totally involved in something that interests you	✦ see new ways of doing things
✦ work well with other people, ask for help, and talk through problems with others	✦ come up with creative solutions
	✦ see long-term implications of things
	✦ can see the total picture
✦ enjoy writing freely – as it comes	✦ are unhurried, don't get in a flap
✦ will try any new idea or technique	✦ listen to others and share ideas
✦ like taking risks generally	✦ see connections between different subjects being studied
✦ work quickly and get others involved and enthusiastic too	✦ present work in novel and artistically appealing ways
✦ like variety and excitement	
✦ are not concerned about making a fool of yourself by asking questions or volunteering for something new	✦ are good at coming up with new alternatives
✦ learn by talking with other people	✦ pinpoint important new questions
✦ skip-read books	

Theorist	*Pragmatist*
You:	You:
✦ organize facts and material well	✦ work well alone
✦ see links between ideas	✦ are good at setting goals and making plans of action
✦ like to understand everything you are working on	✦ know how to find information
✦ are curious, and enjoy problems	✦ see the applications of a theory
✦ work things out well on paper	✦ get things done on time
✦ work well alone with minimum help from teachers and friends	✦ don't get distracted
✦ are precise and thorough	✦ have revision timetables and work plans
✦ plan well in advance for essays and exams	✦ organize time well and have time for other things
✦ set clear goals, know why you are doing something, and which topic is of the highest priority	✦ read instructions carefully
	✦ research examination papers thoroughly
✦ rework essays and notes	✦ have notes classified and filed
✦ are a good critic	

Table 1.5 Disadvantages of Each Learning Style

Activist	*Reflector*
You:	You:
◆ don't plan work in advance ◆ rush into examination questions and essays without thinking them through ◆ tend to neglect subjects you're not interested in ◆ are not good at organizing time ◆ try to do too many things at once ◆ are not good at working out priorities ◆ leave things until the last minute ◆ can be demanding of friends ◆ can't be bothered with details ◆ don't read through or check work ◆ don't rework notes or classify material	◆ can't see the 'trees for the wood' – forget important details ◆ wait too long before getting started ◆ can be uncritical of ideas ◆ don't organize work well ◆ don't like work or revision timetables ◆ only work in bursts of energy ◆ forget to bring key books, etc. for homework ◆ are easily distracted from the job in hand ◆ don't rework notes or classify material ◆ are too easygoing, not assertive enough with friends or teachers

Theorist	*Pragmatist*
You:	You:
◆ need too much information before getting down to work and allowing yourself an opinion ◆ are reluctant to try new approaches ◆ can get bogged down in theory ◆ like to do things in a set way – uncreative ◆ don't trust feelings, your own or others' ◆ don't function very well in group discussions ◆ keep problems to yourself ◆ only trust logic ◆ are overcautious, don't like taking risks	◆ are impatient with others' viewpoints ◆ think there is only one way of doing something – your way! ◆ fail to use friends and teachers as resources ◆ 'can't see the wood for the trees' ◆ get preoccupied with details ◆ lack imagination ◆ are poor at coming up with new questions ◆ often don't work well with others ◆ are more concerned with getting the job done than with making sure it's really a good job ◆ cut corners ◆ are not very interested in presentation of your work

Short Review of Learning Styles and Theories

There has been a recent upsurge of interest in student learning styles. Much of this has been concerned with a need to understand the different ways students learn and the strategies that can be devised both to suit individual needs and to improve the effectiveness of student learning generally.

Learning styles are best understood as the characteristics which a student brings to studying and learning situations. These characteristics have evolved over time as a result of both the individual's experiences and personality.

Holistic/serialist approaches

Research by G. Pask ('Styles and strategies of learning', *British Journal of Educational Psychology*, 1976, no. 46, pp. 128-48) showed that many students adopt one of two approaches to learning when faced with new problems. These were termed the holistic and the serialist approaches.

A holistic approach tends to overview the situation, attempting to gain a broad outline of the problem before fitting in the details later. The serialist uses the opposite approach, coming to terms first with the details, then building up a complete picture through a step-by-step approach.

Under experimental conditions it was shown that large differences between the two exist and a student who uses one approach can be disadvantaged if information is provided solely in the opposing style.

Having said that, it is important to recognize that learning situations and much current higher education require both holistic and serialist approaches. Certainly, you will need to develop skills in applying both 'top-down' and 'bottom-up' approaches.

Experiential learning

D. A. Kolb (*Experiential Learning*, Englewood Cliffs, NJ, Prentice-Hall, 1984) developed a model for understanding how students effectively learn from experience. Put simply, students carry out learning activities and are then encouraged to reflect on the activity and develop theories based on these reflections which can be applied in future activities.

Many programmes in further and higher education adopt an 'experiential learning' model. It is a good idea for you to understand the theory behind this approach. You will then be more effective in understanding and predicting lecturer expectations.

Kolb sees effective experiential learning as resulting from students following a four-stage learning cycle, which is shown in Figure 1.1. Kolb's model is based on the cross-comparison of two dimensions. The first deals with the structure of the brain via left-/right-handedness and the second deals with personality through introversion/extraversion. Kolb tends to use technical terms for each of the four points on the learning cycle, but these can be understood as feeling, watching, thinking and doing.

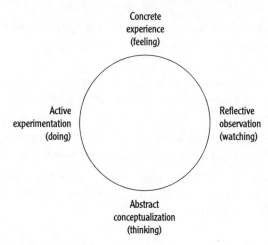

Figure 1.1 Kolb's Experiential Learning Cycle

Feeling (concrete experience) – this involves learning through the feelings developed when undergoing specific experiences. Thus learning takes place by being immersed in the problem, and relies more on intuition than logic. At this stage one does what 'feels right', based frequently on feelings developed when undertaking similar activities in the past.

Watching (reflective observation) – this involves careful consideration of previous experience, or watching, listening and careful reflection before taking action. Hence it is necessary to reflect upon experiences and feelings so as to formulate expectations for the future.

Thinking (abstract conceptualization) – learning at this stage involves analysis of the problem and the application of reflections so as to develop theories for the future. Often this will depend on logical thought, modelling and the development of hypotheses to be tested in the next stage.

Doing (active experimentation) – learning at this stage involves the application of thoughts and ideas. It involves learning through trial and error, developing and amending theories to suit the situation. Clearly, this creates a new set of experiences from which feelings are gained and the cycle commences again.

Bearing in mind the individual personality and tendency to use the left- or right-hand sides of the brain, a person is likely to have preferences for any one of these stages in the learning cycle. Hence it is possible to apply a test (similar to the Honey and Mumford test used previously) which will identify these preferences. Kolb uses different terms, but the broad thrust of each style is similar. A more detailed description is given in Figure 1.2, but briefly the four styles are as follows.

Accommodator: those who learn best by doing and feeling, i.e. by experimentation and concrete experience. They are described in

Accommodator	Feeling	Diverger
Learns best by doing and feeling. Relies more on intuition than on analysis. Needs to know practical application of knowledge. + Works well with others. Will try new ideas. Likes variety and excitement. − Rarely plans activities. Rushes into answering questions.		Learns best by undergoing experiences and then reflecting on them. Needs to be personally involved. Perceives information concretely and processes it reflectively. + Often sees new ways of doing things. Has creative ideas. Sees total picture and connections between topics. − Forgets important details; 'can't see the wood for the trees'. Can be uncritical of ideas.

Doing ── Watching

Converger		Assimilator
Learns best by thinking and doing. Has a strong need to know how things work. Needs hand-on experience, enjoys problem-solving. Is skills oriented. + Good at setting goals and making plans of action. Sees the application of theory. − Tends to see only one way of doing things. Not good as a team worker. Unimaginative.	Thinking	Learns best by watching and thinking. Feels most comfortable when theorizing, developing models and hypotheses. Perceives information abstractly and processes it reflectively. + Organizes facts and materials well. Sees links between ideas. Works well alone with minimum help from others. − Needs too much information before starting work. Does not use others as a resource. Can be uncreative.

Figure 1.2 Kolb's Learning Styles

the top-left quadrant of the diagram. They are most comfortable doing things and rely more on intuition rather than analysis.

Diverger: those who have to undergo concrete experiences and then reflect on these experiences. That is, feeling and watching are the most preferred activities. The description of their style is in the upper-right quadrant.

Assimilator: those who learn best by watching and thinking. They feel most comfortable when theorizing, developing models and hypotheses. They are described in the lower-right quadrant in the diagram.

Converger: these are students with a strong preference for thinking and doing. They are chiefly interested in the practical application of ideas. They are described in the lower-left quadrant.

> REMEMBER: the most effective learning occurs when you actively move round the experiential learning cycle.

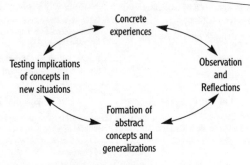

Figure 1.3 The Cycle of Experiential Learning

Deep learning/surface learning

Over recent years there has been growing interest in the strategies which students adopt in learning. A number of studies have suggested that there are two broad strategies which students adopt. There is a distinction between those for whom learning is 'meaningful' (deep) and those for whom it is rote (surface).

Surface learning is associated with an instrumental approach to learning. Here the student sees learning as a chore to be undertaken in pursuit of some desired goal – qualification and job. In this case, the approach is generally concerned with an attempt to minimize the effort required and is directed chiefly at the tasks to reach the goal. Hence success in assessment is the dominant concern and the student does the minimum amount of learning needed to achieve the task. Frequently, these students regard learning as being about memorizing information for later reproduction to satisfy assessment criteria. They rarely reflect on the purpose of learning or how they might learn most effectively. Whilst there are individual differences at work here, there are also situations where a surface approach to learning is a consequence of over-assessment. Students who are required to rush

12 STEPS TO STUDY SUCCESS

from one assessment task to another may have little time for reflection.

The deep approach to learning is used by students who seek to make sense of what they learn. They tend to regard knowledge as important and valuable in itself. They actively follow up learning by setting new information against what they know already. They evaluate information and evidence against conclusions. They actively question during the learning process. They examine the logic of arguments, the supporting evidence, the methods and theoretical underpinning of conclusions. For these students, assessment is not an end in itself but a valuable part of the learning process. For them, assessment both assists learning and helps them sum up what they know. Assessment, therefore, provides a base upon which further personal development takes place. In other words, 'real learning' is by definition 'deep'.

Revision and Review

✓ Learners are involved in an active exploration of experience.

✓ Learners selectively reflect on their experience in a critical way, rather than take experience for granted and assume that the experience on its own is sufficient.

✓ Learners must be committed to the process of exploring and learning.

✓ There must be scope for the learner to exercise some autonomy and independence from the teacher.

✓ Experiential learning is not the same as 'discovery' learning. Both content and process may be determined by the teacher.

✓ Experiential learning involves a cyclical sequence of learning activities.

The Process of Learning

In this step you will consider:

✓ *Some basics about the brain*

✓ *Memory and recall*

✓ *Attention span and concentration*

✓ *Anxiety and performance*

Some Starting Questions

→ During your time at school and college has anyone ever taught you about how your memory functions?

→ Were you ever taught anything about concentration and how to maintain it when necessary?

→ Were you ever given any instruction in how the brain works and how you can use its capacities effectively?

→ Were you ever told about the nature of keywords and key concepts and how they relate to note-taking and imagination?

→ Were you given instruction in thinking and creativity?

Spend a few minutes thinking about your past study experiences and note down the way you go about learning.

The Brain

When people talk about their capacities to learn they often make reference to their mental capacities and brain power as though there are finite limits to these.

'I'm no good at maths or accounts.'
'I can't learn any more.'
'I'm not very bright.'

All of these statements assume that somehow their brain, mind or ability to learn has some 'natural' limit. Nothing could be further from the truth. Scientists have not been able to come up with a real understanding of how the brain works. Yet what they do know is that the brain is extremely complex and grossly under-used.

→ The average brain contains some 10,000,000,000 neurons or nerve cells.

→ This produces an estimated number of connections which could be expressed as 10 to the power of 800.

→ There are between 100,000 and 1 million different chemicals at work in the brain.

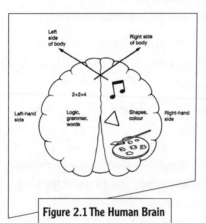

Figure 2.1 The Human Brain

Most people who have difficulties in learning at school or college have not been taught how to learn and their difficulties have little to do with their 'natural' abilities.

Here are some reasons why people find learning difficult:

◆ *they don't understand the learning process and don't use themselves properly*

◆ *they don't organize their time properly*

◆ *they have low motivation to learn*

◆ *they are influenced by family and friends*

◆ *they have low expectations*

◆ *they learn to fail*

◆ *they fail to understand the requirements of the teacher or lecturer*

Over recent centuries it has been assumed that the human brain works in a linear way – in other words, in a left-hand-side sort of way. This was related to two main methods of communication: speech and print. Thus most people have been trained in school and college to take notes in sentences or vertical lists because of these assumptions about the brain. Recent evidence has established that the brain is far more multi-dimensional and does not deal with information in received lists.

Consider your own mental processes whilst you are speaking to another person. Similarly the listener is undergoing a complex of processes as he/she analyses the words and the contexts within which the words or messages are being uttered.

Concentration and Memory

It is known that people are able to understand material more easily if they have some prior knowledge of the topic, or the information has particular interest or significance to them.

Thus tests show that students who are told that a set reading contains a number of themes are much more likely to detect and remember those themes than students who are given the text to read without any guidance.

Whilst it is unlikely that you will be given such an overview in most of your study, there are implications for your approach to reading texts and in preparation for lectures.

Figure 2.2 shows how recall is likely to happen during any standard learning period – lecture, reading or studying. People are much more likely to recall information from the end and beginning of the session. Things will also be recalled which are of particular significance (A B C), or which are outstanding or unique.

If no set time is given – say, if you are just sitting in the library – the deterioration of recall is even worse.

Structuring study periods where there are planned short breaks, on the other hand, aids recall. Study periods of between

20 and 40 minutes are thought to be the optimal time to spend without a short break. These breaks don't have to be long affairs. A change in activity or just relaxing your body for a few minutes will do.

Figure 2.3 shows how this is likely to have a beneficial effect on recall over the same 2-hour period. The sags in concentration still occur, but because these are in shorter study periods, the loss of recall is less.

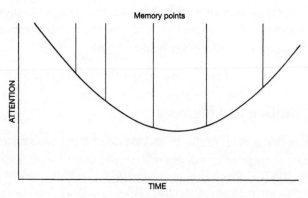

Figure 2.2 Recall During Learning – Unstructured

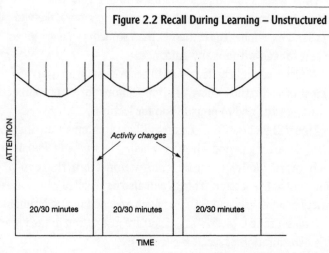

Figure 2.3 Recall During Learning – with Breaks

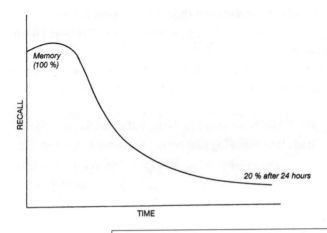

Figure 2.4 Patterns of Recall after a Period of Study

Recall after the learning event is also an important issue. Many students experience learning difficulties not because they don't understand the material in the first place, *but because they fail to prevent forgetting afterwards.* This is undoubtedly one of the major problems in the study of numerate subjects. These subjects require the sequential development of the topic – A has to be understood before B and so on. If students forget A before they get to B, then they have no basis for understanding B: hence the difficulty.

Figure 2.4 highlights the typical pattern of recall after a study session, lecture, library session, etc. Here we see that the amount recalled immediately after the session increases within a short period. This is due to associations and past knowledge adding to the sum of what was remembered. However, from this high point about 30 minutes after the session, the amount recalled generally *declines rapidly over the following 24 hours until about 80 per cent has been forgotten.*

The trick is to maintain what was understood at the high point by regularly reviewing the information. Figure 2.5 shows that the first review should take place within 10 minutes of the study session and last about 8 to 10 minutes. The second review occurs within 24 hours and should take about 4 minutes. After this the review periods need to take only a couple of minutes each time.

The amount recalled will be greater because less information will have been forgotten.

NOTE: Whilst you may find the task of spending part of your study time reviewing your notes from lectures, tutorials and reading of text difficult at first, you will find it is time well spent.

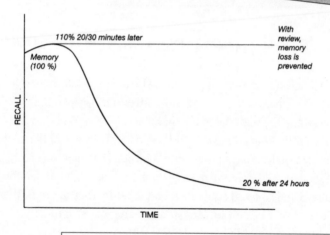

Figure 2.5 How Regular Review Keeps Recall Constantly High

Mnemonics

Memory and recall can also be aided by the use of a range of memory devices known as mnemonics. Most people will have come across some examples provided by teachers or parents to assist in the recall of key facts or dates. For example:

Richard of York Gave Battle in Vain
[His wife was dippy and his brother a pain]
=

Red, Orange, Yellow, Green, Blue, Indigo,Violet
(colours of the rainbow).

Other techniques involve creating visual images of the items to be recalled and locating these in some scene you know well. Others use rhyming lists and inter-linkages between lists of information. It is unlikely that you will be required to remember information in this way, but if you are interested, Tony Buzan's book *Use Your Head* (London, BBC Books, 1974) includes some of these techniques. There is also a host of other texts.

Anxiety and Study

Research on anxiety and performance reveals that some anxiety is required for effective performance – it is necessary to care about success or failure. However, too much anxiety is an inhibitor: it prevents effective performance. Figure 2.6 shows this relationship. As anxiety level increases, performance improves to a point; it then levels off, and as anxiety continues to increase performance begins to decline.

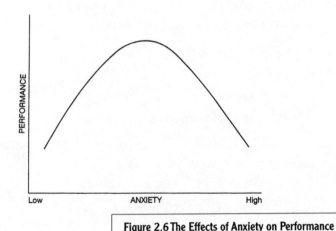

Figure 2.6 The Effects of Anxiety on Performance

Ways to reduce anxiety

◆ *Have confidence in your ability.*

◆ *Know what is expected in the task.*

◆ *Think of success – imagine yourself being successful.*

◆ *Practise the tasks (presentations or examination questions).*

◆ *Spend an appropriate amount of time preparing.*

Revision and Review

✓ It is possible to learn to learn, and most people can improve their performance by adopting systematic approaches to study.

✓ Effective learning uses both sides of the brain.

✓ Understanding and memory will be improved by using pictures and other techniques, which engage the right-hand side of the brain.

✓ Most students can improve on their concentration span by planning their time to include regular changes of activity.

✓ Memory loss can be improved, by frequent review and revision of notes.

✓ Anxiety can be helpful in improving performance, providing it is not excessive and is managed properly.

Organizing Your Study Time

In this step you will consider:

✓ *The need to plan your time*

✓ *How to draw up a study timetable*

✓ *The amount of work which you need to do outside formal class situations*

Why Bother to Organize Your Time?

♦ *Your course is very intense and demands a great deal of effort.*

♦ *You seem to work hard but don't achieve what you expect.*

♦ *You waste time flitting from one study task to another.*

♦ *You take a long time getting started.*

♦ *You spend too long preparing and then have to rush the final assignment.*

Do you recognize any of these problems?
Are there others?

Time management

Managing time as a scarce resource is not just a problem for students. As future employees you will find that coping in a situation where you have conflicting demands on a scarce resource – your time – is a requirement of effective performance in the work-place.

Key steps in time management

➜ Identify those things which have to be done.

➜ Rank these into some sort of priority. This may be in order of importance or in order of time requirements. Essentially decide what has to be done first.

➜ Avoid giving priority to those tasks which you enjoy doing most and putting off those which you enjoy least. This is a common psychological mechanism, enabling the person to feel busy whilst at the same time avoiding that which is uncomfortable.

➜ Sequence the work, giving a realistic time allocation to each activity. Again, it is important that the sequence and time allowed are adhered to, because it is tempting to reduce the time spent on those tasks which are uncomfortable for you.

➜ It is important to recognize that individuals have social as well as task commitments and time needs to be allocated to both these activities.

Some Simple Guidelines in Planning Your Timetable

What to study

Always allocate your time to particular subjects. This will avoid the temptation to concentrate on those subjects which you find most easy. Indeed, it is probably wiser to allocate more time to those subjects which you find difficult.

Having said that, it would be a mistake to allow your strong subjects to suffer because you spent too much time on a weaker one.

You will find the work-load analysis in Table 3.1, on page 50, valuable in this exercise. Remember though that these are estimates of times – you may need to allocate more time than shown.

When to study

It is a good idea to plan your study activities close to the particular lecture, seminar or tutorial. However, the timing of this will depend on which of these activities is involved. It is suggested that you plan study sessions:

♦ *After lectures – so as to allow for review and reflection on the topic, checking your understanding.*

♦ *Before tutorials/seminars – gives you a chance to read background information and prepare to make an effective contribution in the session.*

♦ *Depending on your own temperament – you may find it easier to do primary reading at certain times of the week or day. It is wise to plan these personal requirements into your timetable.*

♦ *Most people find they are freshest in the morning and therefore it is good practice to plan to deal with difficult activities early in the day.*

Using your timetable

Once you have designed the timetable, keep it with you. You may need to refer to it at all times.

♦ *Make a daily list of things to do. This is best written in active verbs, e.g. 'Read and make a summary of chapter 7 in The Skills of Management.'*

♦ *Be prepared to revise your timetable. This is not an exact science; each individual needs to arrive at the patterns of working which are best suited to him or her.*

Figure 3.1 Which of the Above is Likely to be
the Most Effective Studying Position?

♦ *You will certainly need to design a timetable for
each term. You will be expected to spend most time
working on your own and you will need to be well-
organized and self-disciplined.*

Where to study

Whilst it is true that you should be able to study anywhere, most
people need peace and quiet away from distractions. Also, most
people feel comfortable with a regular space – their bit of territory.

Body posture is very important in maintaining your concentration and preventing tiredness. You need space to work at a table
with an upright chair and room to arrange your books and papers.

How Much Time for Study?

The amount of time which you need to spend on study activities
outside of formal lectures, seminars and tutorials will be dependent
on the course you are taking. Is the course full-time or part-time?
Is it designed around a modular structure? Is it based on terms or
semesters? The answers to these questions will influence the
number of hours which you need to allocate to each subject. Having
said that, on all courses, you will be expected to study on your own.
It is highly unlikely that you will be able to successfully complete
the course by just attending lectures and other activities which are
based on contact with tutors.

Table 3.1 Example of a Typical Study Workload

Modules	Lectures	Seminars	Tutorials	Total Contact	Independent Learning	Total Workload
Module 1	15	15	6	36	64	100
Module 2	15	15	6	36	64	100
Module 3	15	15	6	36	64	100
Module 4	15	15	6	36	64	100
Module 5	15	15	6	36	64	100
Module 6	15	15	6	36	64	100
Semester Totals	90	90	36	216	384	600
Weekly Average	6	6	2.4	14.4	25.6	40

NOTE: These are estimates of the average workload involved in each of the modules studied throughout the course. Some students will need to spend more time on the various activities, some may spend less. However, you should plan your week around each of the component elements.

Using the model timetable in Figure 3.2, plan out your weekly activities for your first semester or term.

The above example is based on a typical first degree or higher national diploma programme. These courses are usually planned round an estimated student workload of 1200 hours of study for each academic year. Most academic timetables also assume 30 weeks in each academic year. The weekly student workload, therefore, is estimated at 40 hours of study per week, inclusive of formal class contact.

12 STEPS TO STUDY SUCCESS

The example in Table 3.1 is taken from a course based on the study of six modules over each of two semesters – 12 modules per year. Given the model above, each module is assumed to involve 100 hours of study in each semester. Furthermore, each module in this course is equally weighted in terms of class contact. Where courses include workshop time, specialist training facilities such as kitchens or language laboratories, etc., these times and the balance between class contact and independent study time will alter.

There are a number of activities which make up student workload. Firstly, there are those activities which are formally planned via the course team and involve contact with lecturers and the use of college/university facilities. These are discussed more fully in Session 6, and include lectures, seminars/workshops and tutorials. Typically, these might account for 30 to 45 hours in each module over a semester (2–3 hours per week). Secondly, there are those activities which are based on independent study. These include time spent preparing for lectures, seminars and tutorials, time spent on personal development in expanding knowledge of the subject, and time spent in preparing for various assessed activities.

Daily Action Lists

As well as these devices for planning your weekly timetable, it is also a good idea to give yourself a daily action list of tasks you wish to be completed by the end of the day. These need to be realistic and allow time for things to go wrong. Try not to be over-ambitious. These are techniques to help you to use your time effectively.

Over ambitious targets can create stress because you are always under pressure to complete an impossible workload.

Much of the foregoing may seem mechanistic and over-detailed, but time management is an important skill, both whilst you are a student and later in your working life. The disciplines suggested here are ones which will be most helpful in allowing you to devote sufficient time to your studies and to the many other interests and demands which you will have on your time.

	9–10	10–11	11–12	12–1	1–2	2–3	3–4	4–5	5–6	6–7	7–8	8–9
Mon												
Tue												
Wed												
Thur												
Fri												
Sat												
Sun												

Figure 3.2 Study Timetable

Table 3.2 Time Planning

Time available per week

24 Hours × 7 days   =   168 Hours per week

Complete the list below

Sleep   =

Eating   =

Travel   =

Sporting Activity   =

Leisure   =

List other weekly activities which make demands on your time

                                   =

                                   =

                                   =

                                   =

                                   =

       Weekly total   ____

Revision and Review

✓ Your course will require you to work outside of formal class or lecturer contact.

✓ You will need to plan your time.

✓ Time-management techniques can help you to use your time effectively.

✓ Produce and use a timetable.

✓ Daily action lists help you to focus on the priorities.

Reading Skills

In this step you will consider:

✓ *How to select the reading approach most suited to your study task*

✓ *How to use the SQ3R approach to reading*

✓ *How to increase your reading speed*

Some Starting Questions

Given the intense nature of the course, you will be required to read many books and articles relating to major study areas on the course. As with other aspects of study behaviour, your time will be used more effectively if you approach these tasks in a systematic way.

Some 350 years ago Francis Bacon said,

Some books are to be tasted, others to be swallowed and some few to be chewed and digested; that is, some books are to be read only in parts, others are to be read but not curiously [i.e. not carefully], and some few to be read wholly with diligence and attention.

(quoted in D.A. Rowntree, Learn How to Study, London, McDonald & Jane, 1970, p. 39)

This approach is still useful as it indicates that you should use different techniques depending on your needs. Are you trying to:

→ Check on a specific research question or reference?

→ Get a broad, overall picture of a subject?

→ Gain a detailed, organized knowledge of all the essential facts and ideas on the subject?

Your reading strategies need to be flexible so as to allow for these different needs. The following method has been particularly useful.

SQ3R

Survey
Question
Read
Recall
Review
Survey

Survey

Many people who are given a new book start reading the text without making any attempt to gain an overview of whether the book is worth spending time on.

It is important to survey the whole before you attempt to read the parts. Here are a few suggestions as to how you should gain this overview.

Title page: this can give the answer to some important questions; the general subject area, the level of approach, the author's name and qualifications, the year of publication.

The table of contents: this gives you information about the scope of the book, the way it is organized, and the main chapters and sections. It is a very valuable source of information in sign-posting the issues to be raised.

The index: turning to the back of the book and glancing through the index can be a more detailed source of information about the book. This is particularly useful if you are looking for references on a specific topic.

The preface: the Preface, Author's remarks, Foreword or Introduction will often give you an overview of the writer's intention and assumptions. This can be particularly valuable where there are different views on a topic – often the case in social sciences.

Leaf through the book: turn each page, looking at section headings, any chapter summaries or keywords. Look at any pictures or figures and tables – these can be useful.

Surveying a chapter: having gained an overview of the book, you may wish to look at one chapter in greater depth. Even if you are just dipping into a particular chapter in preparation for a tutorial you should adopt the same approach.

Read the first and last paragraphs: often these will summarize the key points being made. Some of the better textbooks will have chapter summaries or a list of key points or concepts being developed. Headings and sub-headings are also valuable in setting the scene.

Having surveyed the book you are ready to move to the second stage.

Question

The survey process will have helped you to develop further the questions which you want answered. Never start detailed reading until you have some clear question requiring an answer. As we saw earlier, questioning is a vital stage in assisting with recall. These questions will vary according to your tasks, but some issues are probably common. For example:

→ How does this text fit in with what I know already?
→ Who is telling me this?
→ When was this written?
→ What can I do with the information?

The key point is that questioning helps you to read with a purpose. It helps you to be alive to the things being said.

Read

Reading in detail is therefore the third step not, as many students seem to think, the one and only stage. In planning your reading remember some key points:

➔ Reading with a purpose is more effective.

➔ Make reading an active process; in other words you are actively in search of information.

➔ Bear in mind the points about attention span and divide your reading into manageable sections. Don't try to read too much at once.

➔ Make notes after you have read a particular section. Don't try and make notes as you go. This interferes with your ability to question and concentrate.

➔ Look for the idea behind each paragraph. There should be one sentence in the paragraph which sums up the key idea.

➔ Look for the author's plan (Figure 4.1). What is the main idea? How does the author develop the idea behind the book, through each chapter, section and paragraph?

➔ Read the passage again – you may find it easier to return to the book the next day. Difficult concepts will then appear less difficult. Don't expect to understand everything on the first reading.

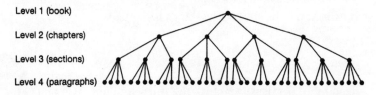

Level 1 (book)
Level 2 (chapters)
Level 3 (sections)
Level 4 (paragraphs)

Figure 4.1 The Author's Hierarchy of Ideas

12 STEPS TO STUDY SUCCESS

Recall

Using the SQ3R method, studying doesn't end with reading the book. You may understand the text, but will you be able to recall it?

> **Most people forget 50 per cent of a book within seconds of putting it down**

Organized recall strategies will improve your learning in a number of ways:

+ *You will concentrate because you have a task ahead of you.*

+ *You can correct memory lapses, thereby making your learning more effective.*

+ *You will be active during the learning process. Again, this will make you much more effective.*

Key steps

→ Depending on the text, try to recall the key points made by each paragraph within a section.

→ Jot down the keywords.

→ It can be useful to try and recall the main explanatory sentence in each paragraph.

→ You are likely to need to spend 50 per cent of your study time recalling what you have read. This may sound excessive but remember – most study problems are caused by forgetting, not by difficulties in understanding in the first place.

Review

Always check the accuracy of what you recall by viewing again the material you have studied. The best way of doing this is to repeat the process, in other words:

◆ *Survey*

◆ *Question*

◆ *Re-read*

◆ *Recall*

Improving Your Reading Skills

Faster reading

The average adult reads at about 240 words per minute, yet most could read 360 words per minute without losing comprehension. You can increase your reading speed in the following ways:

◆ *Reduce the number of fixations.*

◆ *Increase the recognition span.*

◆ *Decrease the number of regressions.*

◆ *Reduce the number of words said to yourself (vocalized).*

◆ *Build up your vocabulary.*

Regular reading

One way to improve your reading speed is to increase your comprehension and expand your word power through regular reading of books, newspapers and journals. The daily broadsheet newspapers (for example, in the UK, *The Times*, *Guardian*, *Independent*, *Financial Times*, *Daily Telegraph*) are a good source of information and help to build your reading skills. As part of your own personal development you should be reading one of these newspapers on a daily basis.

Test Your Understanding

Could you write a sentence for each of these words that would clearly show its meaning?

complacent	deducible	scrutinize
reticence	atrophy	inherent
inertia	lucid	dubious
artefact	precursor	rationalist
dissemination	intractable	propinquity
articulated	infallible	indigenous
paradoxical	insidious	unctuous
jeopardy	banality	envisages
ubiquity	statutory	disparagement
proliferate	disparity	efficacy
synthesis	collate	abject
tentative	intrepidly	concomitant
unimpeachable	spectrum	altruism
aberration	discern	indolence
empirical	immune	inexorably
autonomous	desultory	categorically
tenable	anomaly	cavilling (at)
abstruse	affluent	precipitate (adj.)
eradicate	infer	depravity
ostensibly	authentic	exponents (of)
intuitively	adjacent	sceptical

Count the number of words whose meaning you do not know.

Most courses of study will require you to regularly read articles and books in support of your course. Session 3 suggested that a large part of your time as a student will be spent on activities which rely on independent learning. Much of this is likely to require effective reading skills and the use of sources of information which are written in a style which you would not normally read. Access to this information will need practice and focus. You will find that a systematic attempt to improve these skills and your approach to reading will be helpful.

Revision and Review

✓ The way you read needs to change according to the purpose of your study task.

✓ Survey the whole text before reading the parts.

✓ Question what you already know and what it is you want to gain from the text.

✓ Read with a purpose.

✓ Actively work to improve your recall.

✓ Review what you can recall.

✓ Take steps to improve your reading speed.

✓ Improve your word power.

Making Notes

In this step you will consider:

✓ *The reasons for making notes*

✓ *The needs of an effective note-making system*

✓ *How to use different techniques for making notes*

✓ *The note-taking techniques most suited to your tasks.*

Failure to make and keep adequate notes is a major cause of student learning difficulties. This is not just a problem for the student who does not take notes. Indeed students who write 'everything' down and have massive folders of notes are in equal difficulties.

The Reasons for Making Notes

It is sometimes easy to gain the impression that student note-making is driven as much by cultural considerations as it is by practical, functional purposes. Many students seem to make notes because that is what students do. There seems to be little consideration of the purposes to which the notes are to be put.

Reference

Notes taken during lectures, tutorials and seminars, or from the reading of books and other literature, can provide a valuable source of reference.

> **To be effective such notes need to be easily accessible, stimulate memory and be interesting to review.**

Preparation

In preparation for lectures, seminars and tutorials, as well as working towards the production of essays, reports and presentations, notes will help to organize your ideas and questions for clarification.

It is likely that the purpose to which the notes are to be put will influence the methods you employ in making your notes. This will be dealt with later.

Aiding recall

Through active involvement during a study activity, note-making aids the retention of material and recall. The process of reorganizing ideas and concepts in your own words is in itself likely to aid recall and long-term memory.

Organizing knowledge

Note-making is a valuable way of establishing 'patterns' in knowledge, showing inter-relationships, and the number of points or issues there are to cover in a particular topic. Often the development of a 'map' of the topic is the key to understanding it.

Needs of a Note-making System

Whilst each individual will need to adopt the system of note-making which is the most appropriate to him/her, there are some general considerations to be borne in mind.

Ease of review

Given the need to review material to aid recall, your note-making system should enable you to quickly review the notes you have made on a regular basis.

In some cases students use methods which enable review on an almost sub-conscious level, for example by having notes displayed on bedroom walls.

Flexibility

However you keep notes, the system needs to be capable of change and amendment. Most students find a ring binder, which allows notes to be added and removed, is a useful device.

For some purposes, say for examinations or presentations, where students need to recall information quickly and require a good overview of the topic, large sheets of paper with the information displayed on it in keyword form help to establish the subject in the memory.

Taking account of the brain

As we saw earlier, the brain is capable of taking in information and learning in many forms. The brain doesn't necessarily learn best in linear form with excessive verbiage.

How to Read Better and Faster

Few college students have learned to read as well as they might: they read too slowly, they can't concentrate, and they don't remember what they have read. But they can usually improve by following some of these suggestions.

For improved comprehension, you should apply the SQ3R approach, which will be *active and purposeful*. You should look for the topic sentence (usually the first or last) in each paragraph, for it will carry the *paragraph's main idea*. You will also need to look for the *important details* (examples, proofs, etc.) that support the main idea. (Usually there is at least one important detail to every main idea.) In the search for main ideas and important details you should be alert for visual and verbal *signposts* (clues to the author's meaning) and should pay proper attention to all charts and tables and diagrams. You should not skip over difficulties. Aim to *evaluate* the text by reading sceptically and looking for applications of what is read.

Most people could increase their reading speed by 50 per cent without loss of understanding. During reading, the eyes move across the page from left to right in a series of quick jerks with stops (called *fixations*) in between: during the fixations, the brain registers a group of words (*recognition span*). Poor readers have small recognition spans and therefore make many fixations. They also take many backward glances (*regressions*) over what they have already seen, and they sometimes tend to mouth the words or say them aloud. All these faults help to slow them down.

You can usually improve both speed and understanding in reading: wear reading spectacles if necessary, stop saying words aloud, try consciously to read faster, read in thought units, and *increase your vocabulary*. Vocabulary can be increased by wide reading, learning Greek and Latin word roots, taking note of new words, using the dictionary and making glossaries in specialist subjects. Practice is essential and can be applied both to normal study reading and to regular nightly sessions. In these nightly sessions (half-hour minimum) you should read articles of known length, time how long this takes, calculate speed in words per minute, and then test understanding of the content. Once you have increased your ability to read at speed, you will be able to vary your reading speeds to suit material and purpose: faster perhaps with novels, biography and history and when looking for main ideas; more slowly with instructional manuals and when looking for important details.

Figure 5.1 Summary Notes on Improving Reading Speed

Note-making systems which use colour, shapes, images, humour and patterns are more likely to use the full range of the brain's capacities.

Methods of Making Notes

Summary

The method used in an unsystematic way by many students involves writing a summary of the key ideas or points made in a particular passage. Figure 5.1 is an illustration of this method.

The main advantage is that this encourages thought about the subject and thereby aids learning and recall. The notes may also be useful for explanation.

The major disadvantage is that the notes tend to be over-wordy and thereby difficult to review. Essential points are locked up in excessive verbiage.

Outline notes

Here you make notes shaped by the author's plan – in other words, as though you were trying to reproduce the scheme by which the author wrote the chapter or section.

There is a hierarchy to such note-making:

Main items	Roman numerals (large)	I, II, III, IV
2nd order	Capital letters	A, B, C, D
3rd order	Arabic numbers	1, 2, 3, 4
4th order	Lower-case letters	a, b, c, d
5th order	Roman numerals (small)	i, ii, iii, iv

Move down the hierarchy of ideas from sections through sub-sections to paragraphs. Figure 5.2 illustrates this note-making system.

The main benefit of this system is that it provides a linear list of the key points and their inter-relationship, order of importance, etc.

The main disadvantages are that it is linear, doesn't allow for additional information, and doesn't use the full range of the brain's ability.

How to Read Better and Faster

I. Despite 'experience' few college students read as well as they might (too slow, can't concentrate, forget).

II. For better reading (improved comprehension):

   A. Apply SQ3R to get sense of purpose.

   B. Look for topic sentence in each paragraph:
      1. usually first or last sentence;
      2. contains the *main idea* of the paragraph.

   C. Look for important *details*:
      1. e.g. proof, example, or support for main idea;
      2. usually at least one to each main idea.

   D. In hunt for main ideas and important details:
      1. Watch out for signposts:
         a. visual (layout and type styles);
         b. verbal (clue words and phrases).
      2. Study all charts and tables.
      3. Don't skip difficulties.

   E. *Evaluate* the text:
      1. Be sceptical (expect author to prove).
      2. Look for applications in your own experience.

III. Towards *faster* reading (most people could read half as fast again and still understand just as well).

   A. During reading:
      1. Eyes jerk left to right in series of fixations.
      2. At each fixation, brain decodes group of words.
      3. This makes up its *recognition span*.

   B. *Poor* readers:
      1. Have small recognition spans.
      2. Therefore make many fixations.
      3. Regress frequently (backward glances).
      4. Read aloud (or make sub-vocal noises).

IV. To improve reading (speed and understanding).

    A. Five basic steps:

        1. Check whether you need specs.

        2. Stop saying words aloud.

        3. Consciously try to read faster.

        4. Read in thought-units (2 or 3 words at a time).

        5. Build up vocabulary (reading, speaking, writing) by:

           a. reading widely;

           b. learning Greek and Latin roots;

           c. noting new words;

           d. using dictionary;

           e. making glossaries.

    B. *Practice* (absolutely essential) by:

        1. Nightly sessions (15-30 min.);

           a. read articles of known length;

           b. time yourself (wpm) (Progress chart?);

           c. test your comprehension;

        2. Reading all study material faster.

    C. *Vary* your reading pace:

        1. Faster for 'story-like' material and main ideas.

        2. Slower for complex argument and for important detail.

Figure 5.2 Outline Notes on Improving Reading Speed

Keyword noting

The study of most subjects can be simplified to gaining an understanding of the meaning of a group of keywords. Much of the material written around a topic is developing your understanding of these words and the concepts surrounding them.

Note-making can take advantage of this by focusing on the keywords.

Notes which only use the keywords can get away from linear forms and can use patterns, colour, shapes, humour, etc. Notes

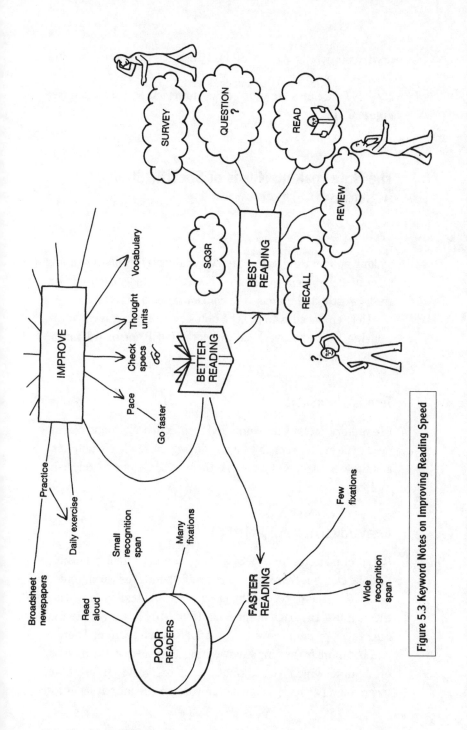

Figure 5.3 Keyword Notes on Improving Reading Speed

taken in keyword form are less bulky because there is less surplus verbiage.

Keyword notes are much easier to review and aid recall (see Figure 5.3).

The Note-making Needs of Specific Study Activities

Lectures

Making notes during lectures is a very valuable way of overcoming some of the problems of lectures. It keeps the student active in the study process and thereby aids concentration and recall.

Here the need is to get the notes down in your own words. Copying from the overhead projector (OHP) or board can be mechanical and a barrier to learning.

Tutorials/seminars

Preparatory notes of key points and themes in background reading need to be easily accessible for use during the session. Quotations and the exact details of particular theories or views are likely to be most useful.

Essays/dissertations/projects

Background notes for a piece of work also need to be accessible, flexible, etc., but there are some specific points to bear in mind.

Notes need to record the exact place and text from whence they came – the page number particularly. Note any potential references or quotations as you analyse each section. There is nothing more frustrating when writing an essay than the memory of a quote which you cannot recall or locate. Information technology, particularly the better word processing packages can be very helpful, because it is possible to make notes and lift quotations directly on to a file which can be called up during the writing process.

Revision and Review

✓ Effective note-taking considers the purpose for which notes are being made; reference, preparation, aiding recall, organizing knowledge.

✓ Note-making systems need to assist in review, be flexible and use both sides of the brain.

✓ Different note-making techniques can assist in improving effectiveness.

✓ Specific study activities, such as in lectures or for tutorials or essays and projects, require note-making systems which support the activity.

Teaching and Learning Strategies

In this step you will consider:

✓ *The purpose, strengths and weaknesses of formal lectures*

✓ *Seminars and tutorials*

✓ *How to gain most from formal lectures, seminars and tutorials*

✓ *How to work effectively in groups*

Teaching and Learning

Much of this text has been directed at giving you advice about how best to learn more effectively, and that has to be your primary concern. However, you are not solely in charge of these processes, in that module tutors and course teams plan the teaching and learning strategies through which they will deliver the programme. The strategies they select, to some extent, set the learning context in which you have to operate. As will be explained later, each of the major class contact situations has flaws as a learning medium, and you need to recognize these weaknesses and approach each situation with a positive attitude which maximizes what you gain from the session. In most courses, it is likely that you will experience three forms of class contact with tutors or lecturers. These are:

The formal lecture
The seminar
The tutorial

In addition you may also work in groups with other students, in both formal and informal situations.

Formal Lectures

Formal lectures are a teaching and learning activity in which a lecturer imparts information to a body of students. Depending on the course, you may find that several of the topics or modules you are studying will include formal lectures given to 80–300 (or more) students in a lecture theatre.

Lectures are attractive from a resource usage point of view because they maximize the economies of scale and appear to use lecturer time efficiently. On the other hand, students frequently complain that the size and scale of lectures make them a poor learning medium. It is important to understand why lectures are used, their benefits and weaknesses, so as to understand how to get the most from them.

Purpose

→ To provide a broad overview of a topic.

→ To introduce students to theories, debates and arguments about a particular topic.

→ To form the basis for further research and study by students in tutorials and seminars, and in their own private study.

Problems with lectures

Whilst lectures have a valuable role to play in your course, the lecture is a problematic medium for teaching and learning. Here are just some of the problems:

✦ Poor teaching mechanism

– no learning by doing

– no learning by discussion

– student attention span

– forgetting

✦ Problem of checking understanding

✦ Problem of maintaining interest

✦ Discipline problems

– talking

– day-dreaming

– not listening

✦ Limited chance to ask and answer questions

Making the Best of Lectures

So as to overcome these difficulties, both lecturers and students have to adopt the right approach. They need to minimize the problems and make the most effective use of lectures.

Lecturers

Don't be surprised if some of your lecturers are not as effective as you might like in the lecture activity. Most have been chosen for their subject expertise rather than their teaching abilities, though ideally it is hoped they are good at teaching as well as being experts in their subject.

Most lecturers will respond to a polite request for a different approach to the lecture, so don't be afraid to ask.

A good lecture, one which will assist you in learning, is likely to contain some of the following features:

◆ *Well-produced visual materials (OHPs) or PowerPoint.*

◆ *Support notes to back up the lecture.*

◆ *Clarity of presentation.*

◆ *Structured presentation:*

  – *introduction outlining what is to be covered*

  – *logical sequence to the material*

  – *a conclusion which reviews the points made*

◆ *Well timed and paced through time allowed.*

◆ *Backed up with material in seminars and tutorials.*

Students

Whilst most lecturers want to be good at what they do, you are ultimately responsible for your own education. You must make the lecture work for you. If you are finding the lecture boring or a waste of time, it is up to you to do something about it.

Here are a few suggestions:

◆ *Prepare for the lecture:*

   – check what is on the topic list

   – prepare questions which you hope the lecturer will answer

   – do some background reading

   – consider last week's lecture

◆ *Make learning an active process:*

   – make your own notes even where the lecture notes are provided

   – question your own understanding.

◆ *Pay attention:*

   – no talking

   – watch out for attention span problems.

◆ *Listen carefully.*

◆ *Use the lecture as the basis for further study.*

◆ *Discuss the lecture with other students:*

   – check each other's notes and share your understanding of the lecture.

♦ *Review your notes over the next few days, weeks and months.*

♦ *Think through the points made over the ensuing week.*

Tutorials

The teaching and learning strategies for most units in your course include a tutorial element. This is defined as a small group situation where 8 to 10 students regularly meet with a lecturer.

Purpose

➜ To enable students to build on their understanding of the topic gained via the lecture and preparatory reading.

➜ To provide an environment in which students can clarify queries and raise questions about the topic.

➜ To encourage discussion and debate between students.

➜ To provide a forum for student presentations and feedback on assessed activities.

Problems with tutorials

There are no inherent problems with tutorials. They are, in principle, an excellent forum for learning. They encourage active involvement and discussion, which stimulates learning. However, there are two major problems which stem from inappropriate behaviour by the participants.

♦ Lecturers talk too much – some lecturers seem to regard the tutorial as yet another lecture. From the learner's point of view this is unlikely to encourage learning because there is little or no student involvement. Sometimes lecturers are forced into this strategy because of the second problem, a failure to prepare by students.

◆ Students fail to prepare for the tutorial. It is difficult to participate in an academic debate if you have not read the necessary background material, nor read through your lecture notes or prepared questions. On an individual basis this denies you the benefit of the tutorial. Collectively, individuals who don't prepare impoverish the tutorial for other students.

Using tutorials effectively

Preparation: prior to each tutorial you must consider the tutorial topic and make an active attempt to prepare for it.

◆ *Read support lecture notes.*

◆ *Read essential reading for the tutorial.*

◆ *Have a look at other texts as well.*

◆ *Raise questions, both for clarification and discussion.*

◆ *Be prepared to make a contribution.*

During the tutorial: each hour is one of only a small number of hours of 'quality' time on the topic. Adopt an approach which maximizes the benefit to you.

◆ *Actively participate.*

◆ *Make contributions, don't wait for others.*

◆ *Raise questions.*

◆ *Make notes of points raised by others.*

◆ *Deal politely with opposing views.*

◆ *Consider how the points being raised add to your own understanding of the topic.*

After the tutorial: don't just close your file for the week, but go back over the points raised in the tutorial.

◆ *Actively recall the points made.*

◆ *Review your notes.*

◆ *Discuss the tutorial with other participants:*

   – check on shared understanding

   – raise questions

   – review each other's notes.

◆ *Question how the material fits into the topic as a whole.*

Seminars

These are used by some subject teams as a way of combining both the lecture and the tutorial. Usually they involve two or three tutorial groups They may include some inputs from lecturers, but this is likely to be less formal than the lecture and include more student involvement.

Purpose

→ To allow a more interactive teaching and learning environment.

→ To enable a closer relationship between lecturer and students than the lecture.

→ To allow for more active participation by students in working through case studies and exercises, as well as presentations by individuals and groups.

Problems with seminars

Again the seminar is not inherently flawed as a teaching and learning strategy, but it can be misused through inappropriate teaching and a lack of student preparation.

The larger numbers in a seminar also mean that individual students can 'hide' or be missed by the lecturer. Obviously it is much more difficult to get to know each individual student than in the tutorial.

These problems are best overcome through the same suggestions raised under tutorials. Essentially you need to:

✦ *Actively prepare for each seminar.*

✦ *Actively involve yourself during the seminar.*

✦ *Actively review the seminar.*

Working in Groups

Group work can be both a source of great satisfaction and support, and a source of frustration and anger. It is important that group members recognize the benefits of working with others, but also realize the pitfalls and difficulties which group work can pose to individual members.

Formal groups

The ability to work effectively as a team member is an essential feature of workplace skills. Employers individually and collectively, and various education bodies such as BTEC and the Management Charter Initiative, all stress the need to work in teams and groups. Courses of study frequently contain group-based exercises both as instruments to assist in student learning and as the forum for assessed activities.

Consequently, it is highly likely that you will be formally assessed in group-work situations. Experience shows, however, that students find this to be a particularly difficult activity which causes much stress both to individuals and between students.

Some frequent problems with group work

+ Group members tend to feel that some members are not making an equal contribution to the group's work.

+ Stress and tension between group members.

+ Individual group members attempt to dominate the group and do not pay attention to the views of others.

+ Group members do not attend agreed meetings.

+ Group members do not complete the work/tasks given.

+ It is difficult for the group to meet because of timetable or geographical reasons.

+ Individual group members cannot meet regularly because they belong to too many different groups.

+ The assessment of group work does not reflect the contributions made by individual members.

◆ Group reports written by different individuals are presented in different styles so the document does not look like one coherent piece of work.

How to overcome the problems

The first step is to meet as a group and discuss your aims and objectives. It is essential that all members agree what is expected of individuals. Here are some suggested areas to cover:

→ How you will be organized – will you elect a chair and/or a secretary?

→ What are your expectations of group members?

→ How will you conduct yourselves?

→ How will you prevent individuals from dominating the group or not doing their fair share?

→ What skills, interests and resources can individual members contribute?

→ Develop a shared understanding of the task in hand – watch out for group think (frozen thinking which excludes other possibilities).

→ Are all members contributing?

→ Are some members dominating?

→ Produce and agree a timetable of meetings or actions which are needed to complete the task.

As the project progresses monitor your performance and ensure that you are working to plan. If there are difficulties, what corrective action is needed?

Once the assignment is completed, are you asked to provide a grade for individual members? Peer group assessment is common on many programmes. Can you justify the grading by arriving at it through objective criteria?

Evaluate your performance as a group once you get feedback from tutors. If you went wrong, where did the errors occur? Was it because of the way you worked as a group? Was it because of a failure to communicate? Did individuals fail to understand what was needed from their contribution?

> **The more time you spend reflecting on your performance as a group, the better prepared you will be for the next exercise.**

Informal groups

Group membership and group formation is a natural and essential feature of all human existence. Whatever the structure of the course and the means by which it is assessed, it is likely that you will meet other students and form informal groups. The informal groups which emerge from the social dynamic of most programmes of study can be a useful source of comfort and support to individual students.

You can use these informal groups to help in study activities in a systematic way by setting up a study group with a small number of friends.

Study groups

Here are a few suggestions as to how you can use a study group:

→ Meet on a regular basis, say weekly or fortnightly, to discuss curriculum issues. Which aspects of the course are giving you difficulties? Is there someone in the group who can help? Are you able to help other group members? Often this process of discussion and mutual explanation can sharpen up everyone's understanding.

→ Arrange a literature discussion. Each person brings a topic to discuss based on the items they have read that week.

→ Discuss assignment briefs and clarify what the lecturers are likely to be after in the assignments. Developing a shared understanding can be very useful. Make sure there is plenty of discussion. Make sure everyone agrees, because sometimes groups can get into 'frozen thinking', which means they develop shared assumptions which exclude inconvenient alternative views.

→ Be careful about the amount of work you do together for assignments, because this can sometimes result in student work which has a familiar feel, even though it has been written individually.

→ Provide each other with feedback from marked work. Sharing pieces of marked work, looking for their strengths and weaknesses, is very valuable. Through this you begin to develop an understanding of standards and expectations.

→ Provide personal support, particularly in the early stages of a programme. You may feel that you are the only person who is finding the subject difficult to understand. Sharing your experiences with others helps in coping, because often these feelings are shared by others.

Many of these suggestions will occur naturally as part of the group dynamic. People will work together with their friends and talk over their experiences. The key here is to make these processes more systematic and a planned part of your study activities.

Revision and Review

✓ Your formal contact with tutors is likely to be through lectures, seminars and tutorials.

✓ Each of these forms of contact can provide learning difficulties and you need to adopt approaches which maximize the learning benefits to you.

✓ A common feature of the best approach is prior preparation and active learning in the session.

✓ Formal group work is an essential feature of many courses. Group work can provide you with organizational difficulties and these need to be overcome with a planned and organized approach to the activities.

✓ Making friends and working in groups is a natural part of student life. These informal groups can be used in a systematic way to support your study.

Gathering Information

In this step you will consider:

✓ *The purpose for which information is sought*

✓ *The information-gathering process*

✓ *Secondary sources of information*

✓ *Primary sources of information*

✓ *Surveys as sources of information*

The Purpose of Information Gathering

Most courses of study require some form of information gathering. Indeed, a defining feature of the educational process is that you develop the tools with which to raise questions and seek out information for yourself. Having said that, different study or assessment tasks will require different sources of information and the approach to information gathering will have to reflect the requirements of the exercise.

In most cases, Francis Bacon's claim that 'knowledge itself is power' holds true. The quality of your study output will reflect the range and quality of information gathered. It is certainly true that weak performance is frequently a consequence of lack of preparation and information gathering. Having said that, too much information gathering can be confusing and bewildering. In some cases, students spend too much time researching the question under consideration and find that they do not know what to do with all the information they have gathered.

The key problem in both cases is that students fail to think analytically about the purpose for which information is to be put and the process for gathering the required information.

Key Questions

Why is the information being gathered? Is the information for an essay or tutorial? Is it for a major dissertation or project? In each case the information required, the sources of information and how the information is to be processed will differ.

What are the aims and objectives? Is the objective to review key theories or concepts? Is it to test out past research or conceptual models? What questions need to be answered?

How will the information be gathered? Will it be by review of sources already published in books, journals or research papers?

Will it be by personal research or by gathering information personally?

Where will the information gathering take place? What are the key information sources? Where will research be undertaken? What restrictions might there be on gaining access to the information? How representative of the range of information available is it?

Who will participate in supplying the information? Will responses from organizations or individuals be required? How will the participants be selected? How representative are they? What difficulties are there likely to be?

How is the information to be processed? How will the information be analysed? Will qualitative or quantitative methods of analysis be used? How will the information be presented? Who will be the audience for the output? What are their information needs? To what use, if any, will the information be put?

The Process of Gathering Information

Bearing in mind some of the common faults in student information gathering discussed above, it is important that you carefully consider how the process of gathering information is to be carried out. Whilst different research tasks will require different techniques, a systematic approach which follows the process outlined in Figure 7.1 can be applied to most information-gathering exercises.

Ultimately, the aim of information-gathering exercises is to answer questions raised by the application of up-to-date, reliable and accurate information. This will be constrained by the time, effort and resources available in the information-gathering process, but careful planning and consideration of the stages

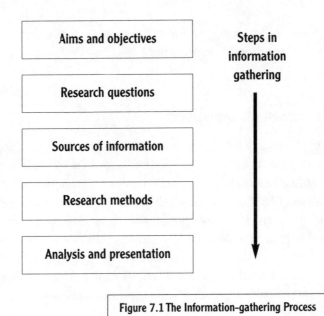

| Aims and objectives |
| Research questions |
| Sources of information |
| Research methods |
| Analysis and presentation |

Steps in
information
gathering

Figure 7.1 The Information-gathering Process

outlined in Figure 7.1 will yield dividends. In some cases, this process can be used as a guide in an informal way without the need to formally create a plan. In other situations, it is advisable to write down a research proposal which acts as a record of the aims, objectives and research questions to be investigated.

Aims and Objectives

The first stage in an information-seeking exercise is to clearly define the problem or issue to be investigated and to come up with some clear aims. These are the final outcome of the research activity. The aims act as a reminder and a guide as to the direction and point of the research process. They are usually written in verbs which express outcomes (determine, explain, examine). The aims shape and direct the objectives for information gathering. They provide immediate targets which have to be achieved as part of the process of achieving the aims. Objectives should be expressed in active verbs (read, interview, produce).

Research Questions

All information gathering must involve attempts to answer questions. Thus, to be effective the process has to be focused on and directed to questions. Even information gathering for your personal development is most effective when located in a framework of questions. The question might be, 'What do I know about this subject?' or 'How does this information contribute to what I already know?' With more formal research projects the questions to be answered need to be laid down. They determine the type of information required, the methods of investigation and sources to be tapped.

Types of Information

The purpose of the information-gathering activity will shape the types of information which need to be collected. This in turn directs the information-gathering exercise to different sources of information and methods of gathering it.

All information can be typified as either being *quantitative* or *qualitative*. Quantitative information is numerical and statistical. It is usually measured through some sort of scale, which means it can be manipulated by a variety of statistical techniques. Hence quantitative information is enumerated, and concerned with frequency and distribution. Qualitative information is non-numerical and may relate to characteristics. It cannot be manipulated via statistical techniques. Often qualitative information is sought when attempting to gather information about people's opinions or the meanings attached to different terms or phenomena.

Different courses of study may require more or less quantitative or qualitative data. Information gathering in social sciences (including most business and management programmes) is likely to require the use of both types of information.

Sources of Information

Information sources are wide and varied, but are usually classified under two broad headings. *Secondary* sources of information already exist and have been gathered by someone else. These will be discussed in detail later, but official statistics, prior studies, journal articles and newspapers are all sources of secondary information. *Primary* sources of information are those from which the researcher gathers information first hand. This might be through a variety of methods clustered in three main styles of research: experimentation, observation and surveys.

The purpose of the information is again important here. Research for an essay or tutorial may well rely mostly on secondary sources, whilst information gathering for a project or dissertation may well require the use of primary sources.

It is important that you start with a search of the secondary sources, even with those exercises which require you to gather primary data, because secondary sources provide a valuable overview of the key issues and questions. In most cases, the breadth of secondary sources used is also important. Social science topics, particularly, are often controversial, the subject of a range of opinions and preferences in the style of information. Your answers will generally require that you reflect this range of styles and theories.

Secondary Sources of Information

One of the first steps you need to take as a student on a new course is to discover the library and information sources available to you. Most college and university libraries are much more than places to store books. They include a wide range of sources of information via printed and electronic media. The sooner you understand the array of information available, the more effective will be your information-gathering activities. Most academic libraries offer induction programmes to assist new students in gaining access to the range of information offered.

In addition to the college or university library, it is worth investigating the public library services available to you. Frequently the main library will have a well-developed reference section, particularly if the topic which you wish to research has local significance, say a local industry, organization or character.

Also locally, you may find that it is possible to have access to library resources in other local colleges or universities. In other cases, the Chamber of Commerce, local employers' groups or trade unions, interest groups, industry bodies or local government offices can be sources of information.

On a national level, many industry or professional bodies produce research reports about trends and developments in the industry. Some have library resources which they will share with students. Others will sell information to non-members. The following list of sources of information is not exhaustive. The precise nature of the information available will depend on the course which you are undertaking and the institution at which you are studying. The key point is that time spent in investigating the information available to you will be time well spent, and better done before you are under pressure to research an assignment.

Government statistics: the government produces a vast amount of information in the form of reports and statistics. You need to make sure that you are aware of the information produced in your subject area.

Private sector research reports: various private organizations produce reports on industries and trends. For example, Mintel and

Euromonitor are a good source of information on various markets. In some cases, banks, accountants or consultants produce industry specific reports on trends and industrial performance.

Industry-specific/professional journals: most industries and occupations have journals which can be a valuable source of information. These will vary from those which are almost newsletters to more academic journals which include items about current research and debates within the field of study. In all cases, you need to regularly review these journals so as to know what information is available.

Newspapers and magazines: the 'broadsheets' (e.g. in the UK, *The Times, Financial Times, Guardian*, etc.) and specialist magazines written for a wider public audience (e.g., in the UK, the *Economist, New Statesman* and *Society*, etc.) can be sources of information. Clearly it is worth considering the credibility of such items, but they can be useful and most libraries will have back copies. Frequently these are supported by some sort of indexing and electronic access systems.

Research registers: some organizations produce research registers which allow access to current research topics and projects within a field of study. Increasingly these sources are available on CD-ROM.

Electronic systems: a variety of ever-expanding sources of information are available through CD-ROM and on-line search systems. It is possible to gain access to a host of articles and journals relating to specific topics. These sources can also yield information for specific purposes, for example, FAME provides access to the published financial accounts of British companies.

References in academic journals and books: in many cases the references used by authors of academic articles and books can provide a source of suggested texts. These can be acquired through the library or from the British Library on inter-library loan.

Some limitations of secondary sources of information

Whilst it is true that secondary sources of information are all that is available to you for some study tasks, it is wise to remember that such sources may have some important limitations.

When was the information gathered? It is worth considering the age of the information source. Is it still relevant? Have circumstances changed?

Who collected and presented the information? Was the researcher/ writer reputable? Are they writing from a particular perspective? One of the major drawbacks of newspapers as sources of information is that they are written with a particular ideology in mind. Similarly, books may well be written with a set of assumptions in mind which provides a limited perspective on the topic.

How was the information gathered? Here issues about research design, sample size, research methods, etc., are important because they might produce a distorted picture. It is possible that flaws in the research design require the results to be treated with caution.

Why was the information gathered? It may be that the information was gathered for a different purpose from the one you propose, with the consequence that the information is not appropriate.

Tests of Information Gathering and Research Activities

When gathering information from both secondary and primary sources, the aim of the exercise is to gather information which is accurate, relevant and up to date. Three concepts are helpful when considering a particular piece of research.

Validity is concerned with the extent that a particular research activity does measure what the researcher intends. Validity is checked through the research process – the research design and the conclusions drawn from the data. Validity reflects upon the extent that a piece of published research can be trusted.

Reliability is concerned with the extent that the research outcomes would be reproduced if they were to be repeated under similar conditions by different researchers. A particular issue in social science research is the extent to which different researchers would arrive at the same findings given similar situations.

Triangulation is the use of different research methods or sources of data to examine the same problem. Most research methods have flaws and drawbacks and so it is often necessary to 'triangulate' the research so that findings are not being influenced by the research methods used. Again, social science research provides particular problems for researchers because human behaviour is complex and it is frequently difficult to isolate single factors which influence behaviour.

The tests of validity, reliability and triangulation are useful ones to apply, both when evaluating secondary sources of information, and when designing primary information-gathering activities.

Primary Sources of Information

Many courses of study require students to engage in some form of primary research activity. The nature of research method-ology and specific research methods is a large topic in itself, and there is not sufficient space in the step to cover all topics completely. If you want more detailed information, studying one of the texts that explore research methods in your field is advisable.

This section will provide an overview of the topic and some detailed advice on the forms of information-gathering techniques most commonly used by students.

Styles of primary research

Experiments are what many people imagine when they think of gathering information in a scientific manner. The experiment is widely used in the physical sciences. It typically involves the isolation of one or more factors (independent variables) which are then altered with a view to examining the consequences for the experimental object and measuring the resultant changes (the dependent variable). Experiments have also been used in the social sciences. Here the principle is the same, though there are debates about validity and reliability because the causes of human behaviour are often difficult to isolate and people frequently behave differently outside of experimental situations.

Experimental research has wide application in both physical and social sciences and is likely to be included in the specific content of particular courses of study. As a general research instrument used in student information gathering, experiments are likely to be used in only a limited number of situations.

Ethnographic research, or research by observing, is a style used in social science research. Initially developed in anthropology, ethnographic research includes a range of techniques which attempt to gain an understanding of human actions and perceptions through the study of behaviour in 'natural' settings. Participant observation, for example, attempts to overcome some of the difficulties of experimental methods by studying people in the situations in which they normally work and make decisions. Whilst advocates of these approaches claim that the resulting information is richer and provides a better understanding of human actions, some researchers prefer the 'harder' information which comes from statistical measures through experiments and surveys. Other criticisms can be made regarding the sample size and cost of this style of research. Again, you may come across secondary sources of data which include ethnographic sources of data, but it is unlikely that you will be in a position to use ethnographic studies in your primary research. One exception might be on a course which involves industrial release. Used properly this could be a valuable way of studying the way people deal with some sensitive issues. For example, attempts to research racial or sexual prejudice in recruitment and selection are understandably difficult, because people frequently act differently than they claim. Observation of decisions in the workplace can reveal more realistic data about actions and views than experiments or surveys.

'Surveys' describes a range of techniques in which the researcher goes out to ask questions of the subjects under examination. This might be in the form of questionnaires or interviews. Usually the person carrying out the survey will ask a pre-determined set of questions of all the people being surveyed. In some cases the survey will ask all the people in the *'population'*. An example here is the Census which is conducted every ten years in the UK. In theory every person is required to be accounted for in the survey and the word census means 100 per cent sample survey. In most cases the *'population'* (all those who might be included in the survey) is too large and the survey is based on asking questions of a *'representative sample'*. Opinion polls are a common example of surveys which are widely used. Here the researcher attempts to gain an insight into voting intentions or impressions of different products through surveys of a sample of voters or shoppers.

The survey is the most common research style which students are likely to use in general courses of study. The following sections aim to outline some of the key issues for you to consider in this form of primary research.

Gathering Information Through Surveys

Surveys can be conducted through a number of methods including various forms of questionnaire and interviews. Each has some specific benefits and limitations. Some of the more widely used examples will be given below. In general, surveys can be characterized as follows:

+ The survey method involves a sample of respondents replying to a number of fixed questions under comparable conditions.

+ Surveys may be administered by a researcher who completes a form on behalf of the interviewee, or on a form which is sent to the respondent for self-completion.

+ Surveys may include interviews with respondents using structured questions or in unstructured formats.

+ Respondents to a survey represent a previously identified population. If all those who make up the population are included in the survey, a census has been taken. In other cases, only a small proportion of the population will be surveyed and this is a sample survey.

+ Sample surveys must represent the population by including within the sample all the variations in the population.

Surveys allow information to be gathered quickly and relatively cheaply. A wide range of information can be covered in a way that other styles of research would not allow. It is possible to survey a much larger number of people than with other styles. Hence the information gathered will be based on a bigger sample of the population than might be possible with observation or experimentation techniques.

A key problem is that respondents frequently do not give answers that reflect their behaviour in life. In some cases they give the answers which they think they ought to give. In other cases they just behave differently when faced with real, rather than hypothetical, choices.

A second problem area is the sampling frame. It may not be truly representative of the population; thus findings are distorted because they do not reflect the population as a whole. Some forms of survey, particularly those using postal techniques, can generate notoriously low response rates frequently as low as 5 per cent of the questionnaires sent out.

Questionnaires

These are very popular research instruments in student information-gathering activities. Frequently, however, they are not well constructed, and tend to over-estimate the willingness of their targeted sample to respond. Like all research methods, the use of questionnaires in gathering information needs to be consistent with the aims and objectives of the research, the questions being explored, and a practical assessment of the resources available for the research.

Postal questionnaires are usually sent to the respondents for completion and return (either by post or collection). At face value they are inexpensive because a large number can be sent out at relatively low cost. However, the return rate is generally low, unless you have previously asked the permission of the respondent. Response rates can be improved if you follow some simple steps.

➜ Direct the questionnaire to a named individual. Better to address it Mrs Brown, Marketing Manager, rather than The Marketing Manager.

→ Keep it short. Responses will be lower if the questionnaire is overlong.

→ Ideally ask the permission of the respondent and ask them to return it by a given date.

→ If you have the time and resources, collect forms personally because people will feel more obliged to complete them. If not, send a stamped addressed envelope.

→ Bear in mind the low response rate and the major limitation of the use of questionnaires, namely that they tend not to allow for two-way communication and clarification.

→ Conduct a pilot study to check how well the questionnaire works.

Telephone questionnaires involve gathering information from respondents by telephone. This can be done as 'on spec', or after having sent a questionnaire to the respondent, say where you require the person to have detailed information. The telephone allows you to overcome one of the major weaknesses of the postal questionnaire, namely it allows for two-way communication. It is possible to clarify points and follow up with other questions where needed.

This form of survey is cheaper and quicker than face-to-face interviews, because travelling time is removed and more respondents can be covered. Response rates tend to be better than with postal questionnaires. Telephone questionnaires are more expensive and time-consuming than postal questionnaires. The use of visual aids may be difficult with this form of survey. Again there are some simple steps which can improve response rates and effectiveness.

→ Try to make contact at times when the respondents will be available, or not busy.

→ It is a good idea to find out the name of the individual to whom you wish to speak, and if the research design allows, contact them first to prepare them.

→ Keep the interview short. Apart from cost, busy people may resent a long telephone call, and consequently be dismissive about their responses.

→ Remember that this survey method has weaknesses where detailed accurate information is needed or where the respondent needs to make visually stimulated choices.

Personally administered questionnaires are usually conducted by an interviewer who is able to complete the responses. In some cases, questionnaires are administered as the result of a pre-arranged meeting, say following from a telephone call. In other cases, interviews are conducted 'on spec' using a sampling technique.

This method allows the use of visual aids, television, radio, or prompt cards where an instant reaction is needed. Administered questionnaires may enable a more structured sample to be constructed, e.g. if you are wanting to interview only people who eat out regularly, it is possible to filter out (and thereby not interview) those who do not. Response rates for this type of survey tend to be quite high, because the interviews are only directed at those who are willing to participate.

Administered questionnaires can be expensive and time-consuming, because they do involve interviewer time to administer. As with other face-to-face survey methods, interviewees may tend to give you the responses which they think you want to hear. Also it is important to think carefully about the sample design, because just stopping people in the street can produce some important distortions.

→ If the interviews have been previously arranged, make sure that respondents know what to expect, namely the purpose of the questionnaire and approximately how long it will take.

→ Make sure the sample is representative of the population. This is particularly the case where 'random sampling', say in the street, is concerned.

→ Make sure that you minimize the influence of your own persona and opinions. Try to avoid body language which either approves or disapproves of responses.

→ Make sure you have the necessary visual aids or 'prompt cards' to hand for the interview.

Types of question

There are a number of different types of question which can be used on a questionnaire. The choice of questions and types asked will be influenced by the aims and objectives of the research and type of information being sought.

Closed questions are questions where it is possible to predict a range of likely answers or where there are only a set number of responses. It is usually advisable to draw these up through a pilot study. This type of question may be used as prompts to avoid relying on respondents' memory, or to avoid potentially embarrassing questions by asking them to indicate their age via preset bands. The advantage of closed-answer questions is that they are easier to analyse, and by using number codes responses can be computerized and subject to statistical analysis.

Example:

How did you travel to the restaurant? (please tick)

- ☐ Own car
- ☐ Taxi
- ☐ Bus
- ☐ Cycle
- ☐ Walk
- ☐ Other (please state)

It is usually a good idea to include a category 'Other' in the list, just in case there are some responses which have not been considered. Allow space for details to be written in. Questions might ask for multiple-choice, or for priorities by ordering them in rank order. It should be clear as to how the respondent is to rank them – high numbers most preferred or least preferred? In an administered questionnaire these responses might be provided on a prompt card.

Open questions allow the respondents to answer the questions in their own words and using their own priorities. Questions which ask opinions about something are frequently asked in this way. A major benefit is that respondents' images and perceptions are more likely to emerge. Answers should be written exactly as used, or taped, because this will reveal the most about respondents' views.

Example:

What new services would you like the restaurant to offer?

A consequence of this type of question is that answers are difficult to analyse and codify, because people use different words and phrases. Frequently, analysis would involve the identification of broad trends, but enclose a copy of each response in the Appendix of the report.

Attitude questions are those where the aim is to discover positive or negative feelings about a particular issue. By converting responses to numerical forms it is possible to produce a statistical analysis of the responses.

There are a number of types of questions which allow for attitudes to be measured. The *Likert Scale* provides a number of attitude statements to which the respondent has to agree or disagree.

Example:

Listed below is a set of statements. Please read each one and indicate with a tick whether you strongly agree, agree, disagree or strongly disagree.

Statement	Strongly Agree	Agree	Disagree	Strongly Disagree
1. The restaurant was clean				
2. The staff were friendly				
3. The food quality was acceptable				
4. My visit to the restaurant was value for money				

The above example uses only four potential responses, the thinking being that respondents are forced to express a general preference. It is also possible to add a fifth category allowing for

'Neither agree or disagree', allowing respondents to record a middling view which may be appropriate for some questions.

A second measure of attitudes is the *Semantic Differential Scale*. Here the strength of attitudes is measured through the pairing of words, with an interconnecting scale upon which respondents register their responses. It is usually advisable to alter the direction of the positive and negative responses, to avoid thoughtless responses which merely continue down one side of the scale.

Example:

Please indicate your attitudes to the restaurant by placing a circle around one of the points between each of these pairs of words. The restaurant was:

Clean + + + + + Dirty

Poor Value + + + + + Good Value

Food Quality Acceptable + + + + + Food Quality Unacceptable

Staff Were Unfriendly + + + + + Staff Were Friendly

The semantic differential scale may also be converted to a numerical measure so that responses can be measured and trends identified. In the example below, the number sequence would follow a consistent pattern, say, low numbers being positive and high numbers being negative.

Clean 1 2 3 4 5 Dirty

Poor Value 5 4 3 2 1 Good Value

Framing the questions

Devising questions for use in surveys is an important skill. The range and type of questions included in the questionnaire will be dependent on the aims of the research and information which you are trying to gather. Indeed, when framing questions it is a good idea to start with a broad outline of the areas of information sought. As you write each question, critically consider how it will contribute to the information which you aim to gather. There are some important points to bear in mind when preparing the questions:

→ If the questionnaire is to be completed by the respondent, commence the questionnaire with a brief statement of the purpose of the questionnaire.

→ Avoid hypothetical questions. Ask questions which the respondent can reasonably answer. Avoid questions which rely on memory.

→ Use words with clear meanings. Do not use words which can have several meanings, or with local variations. For example, 'dinner' can mean different meal occasions in different parts of the country.

→ Avoid phrases which might be interpreted differently. Give respondents clear statements which do not overlap or give the possibility of providing the same answer in several categories.

→ Ask questions which explore a single issue. For example, 'Is the restaurant clean and tidy?' might create confusion if the respondent wants to give a split response – 'It is tidy but not clean'.

→ Keep questions simple. Avoid long complex phrases, or phrases which include double negatives. The guiding principle is that, if people can get it wrong, they will get it wrong.

→ Where choices are to be made by respondents, it is a good idea to provide 'prompts' or 'show cards'. This avoids reliance on respondents' memory.

→ Avoid questions which might lead the respondent into giving the responses which they think you want, or which become ego defensive – for example, if the respondent thinks they ought to answer in a particular way, or ought to know a particular fact.

→ Arrange questions in a logical sequence, exploring themes. Do not arrange questions in a way that flits between topics.

→ Make sure that all instructions to respondents are clear and concise, particularly where multiple-response questions are involved. There should be no ambiguity about how a question is to be answered.

→ Leave personal or sensitive questions towards the end of the questionnaire. You reduce the risk of alienating the respondent whilst gathering the bulk of the information.

→ If you consider a question might be embarrassing or sensitive, ask the respondent to select from bands in a closed question. For example, questions about age or income are frequently asked in this way.

→ Self-completion questionnaires should finish with some polite message thanking the respondents for their time.

You will find that a pilot study will assist in developing the questionnaire. Try the first draft out on some typical respondents and check the questionnaire for difficulties or ambiguities. Amend this first draft in the light of your findings from the pilot study.

Consider the means by which responses are to be collated and analysed. Computer programs, such as SNAP, can be invaluable in both questionnaire design and the collation and analysis of responses.

Interviews

Apart from questionnaires, interviews are an important form of survey. There are a number of different types of interview which can be used for different sorts of information, or which might be used at different stages in the research process. In all cases you will find that tape recording the interview will assist when interpreting the information gathered.

Structured interviews have some features in common with the administered questionnaire. Questions are predetermined and asked in the same way of all respondents. There is likely to be a wider use of open-ended questions which allow the respondent to express their views in their own words. There is an opportunity to expand and develop the responses through two-way communication. The main benefit is having a uniform set of questions aimed at discovering responses to key questions, but which also allows more personal response and the potential for richer data.

Structured interviews will frequently be used with a questionnaire which is completed by the interviewer. In other cases, the interviewer may have a list of pre-set questions which are used as the basis for the interview and the interviewer then makes notes of the responses. Many of the principles which apply to questionnaire design, outlined above, also apply to this type of interview.

Unstructured interviews are largely based around a series of themes which the interviewer wishes to pursue. The interviewer may have a set of topics to cover, but will weave these into the conversation as the interview flows. These interviews will usually yield much more about the respondent's perceptions and views about issues. They are frequently used as a preliminary stage to a wider study, for example, where the researcher wishes to gain an overview of the issues and possible concepts.

Unstructured interviews are based upon open-ended questions which will encourage respondents to give full answers. Avoid questions which will generate yes or no answers. Questions which use words such as who, what, where, when, how and why are most likely to generate responses which are full and yield rich data.

Whilst this type of interview has the advantage of yielding richer data, they are also time-consuming and can be difficult to analyse. Respondents will use different language and concepts in their answers, so data analysis and presentation need to be carefully undertaken.

→ A tape-recorder is an essential aid in this form of interview.

→ Follow up questions where the answer might be ambiguous or unexplained. A supplementary question which asks for an explanation can be useful.

→ Display a genuine interest in what the respondent has to say. People are likely to be open and willing to talk if you seem interested in what they have to say.

→ Watch out for leading questions or body language which suggests to the respondent that you expect, or approve/disapprove of, certain answers.

→ Ensure that the interview is conducted in peace and quiet with no interruptions.

→ It is a good idea to inform the respondent of the purpose of the interview, the topics to be covered and the approximate time it will take prior to the interview.

Analysis of this type of data will frequently require the identification of key themes in responses, but will also include quotations from the respondents. It is good practice to type up the transcripts of these interviews and include these in the Appendix of any report which is produced.

Arriving at the sample

Where the total population of your research target is relatively small it may be possible to gather information from the whole population – for example, if you are conducting research into the attitudes of your fellow course members. In most cases, however, you will not have the time and resources to do this and will need to devise a representative sample. There are a number of different methods by which you can do this. The purpose is to arrive at a sample to be surveyed which, as far as possible, reflects the characteristics of the whole population.

Random samples are constructed through the principle that every member of the population under scrutiny can be included in the sample. Inclusion in the sample is arrived at by chance, either by using some common formula, or more usually by using random tables.

This type of technique is frequently used where difference amongst the population is unknown. By using a random sample, variations amongst the population can be exposed. Random samples may also be used where the population appears to be homogeneous.

Stratified samples are used where the population is known to be split into groups with similar characteristics (strata) whose relative size is known, for example, age groups or socio-economic groups. In these cases the sample may be stratified to reflect the proportions of the population. A random sample may then be taken from within each stratum.

Proportionate sampling involves taking a fixed proportion of each stratum in the population. It may be that the sample takes, say, 5 per cent of the population in each stratum. Often this can be used where the population is relatively small or where there are a limited range of strata – say in types of organizations.

Whichever form of sampling is applied, your information-gathering process needs to consider the construction of the sample very carefully. Even if the research is limited to interviews with a relatively small number of respondents, their representativeness of the population is an important issue in evaluating the validity and reliability of your findings.

Revision and Review

✓ Information gathering is an important part of most courses of study.

✓ Adopt a systematic approach to gathering information which starts with consideration of the aims and objectives of the exercise.

✓ A fundamental first step is to get to know the full range of secondary sources of information available to you.

✓ If you need to conduct primary research, think about the research methods most suited to your purpose.

✓ The types of questions which you ask, either through questionnaires or interviews, must also match the type of information you are trying to gather.

✓ The sample included in the information-gathering process must reflect the characteristics of the population which you are researching.

Presenting Numerical Data

In this step you will consider:

✓ *Types of presentation*

✓ *Ways of presenting qualitative data*

✓ *Ways of presenting quantitative data*

✓ *How best to convert data into information*

Data Presentation

Many projects, reports and investigations which you will encounter on the course will require the analysis and presentation of data. Using numbers to assist in the understanding and in communicating aids and supports the narrative that you develop in your verbal or written presentation.

This step aims to extend your appreciation of the different techniques and show how these can assist in the communication process. It also aims to establish the rules of how to present these in a professional manner.

Types of Presentation

It is necessary to draw a distinction between two basic types of data:

Qualitative or 'type' data: these are data which can be categorized by characteristics, for example, gender [male or female] or whether people own a mobile phone [yes or no]. The key point is that categories discriminate and there is no suggestion of order or preference.

Quantitative or 'size' data: these are data which can be categorized by variables. These are usually measurable against some sort of scale or standard units of measurement, for example speed [miles per hour], sales [£ per hour, transactions per hour], or weight.

Qualitative Data

Tabulation

A summary table is a simple way of presenting qualitative data. It is constructed by showing how many items or people (occurrences in the data) fall into each category. This can be a quick and effective technique which communicates the information in an easily accessible manner. Tables 8.1 and 8.2 are examples of summary tables. Note that there are some important rules about the presentation of both tables (involving columns and rows of numbers) and figures (graphs, charts, etc.) which will be indicated through the text.

Rule 1: When using any form of table or figure in a written document, the topic must be introduced and discussed prior to the table or figure.

Rule 2: All tables most be clearly titled and numbered.

Rule 3: Make sure that all data and categories are clearly labelled. There must be no confusion about the data being presented. Is it actual numbers, as above, or £s, or tonnes?

Rule 4: If data are taken from published material, indicate the source.

In Table 8.1 the attribute is gender, in Table 8.2 it is restaurants, and the data presented show both what the table is about and the units of measurement.

In collating data it is possible that more than one quality or characteristic needs to be compared. A contingency table arranges one quality vertically and the other horizontally. This type of table allows comparison of data so as to examine whether one quality is contingent on, or depends on, the other. Table 8.3 is an example of a contingency table. Here job titles are compared with the gender of the job holders.

Tables provide a useful way of looking at data and gaining a feel for the information. There are several techniques which can be used to present the data in a more dramatic and visually stimulating way.

When giving information in presentations or in written form these techniques can be valuable in aiding the communication process. As stated earlier, they help the reader/audience gain the thrust of the message through pictorial forms which engage the right-hand side of the brain. Hence it is important that you select the techniques which communicate the information most effectively.

> **Rule 5: Select the form of chart which most effectively communicates the image which the data reveals.**
>
> **Rule 6: Locate the table or figure close to the relevant section in the text in order to provide visual support for the written material.**

A *bar chart* can be used to show how qualitative data compare against the various categories which have been established. As with a summary table, bar charts are created by establishing categories entering the units of measurement against each. Bar charts can be presented in a horizontal or vertical form. Figure 8.1 is an example of a vertical bar chart, because the categories are displayed along the horizontal axis and the different units of measurement can be compared by the vertical height of the bars. Here the restaurants are compared in terms of sales revenue in the given month. Thus the height of the bars provides a visual comparison of the sales revenue in each restaurant. These are the same data as were provided in Table 8.2.

> **Consider Table 8.2 and Figure 8. 1. Which communicates most effectively the variations and relative size of each restaurant's sales in December?**

Table 8.1 Composition of the Workforce in Captain Dan's Fish Restaurants (December 2000)

Gender	Number of Employees
Male	93
Female	398
Total	491

Table 8.2 Sales in Captain Dan's Fish Restaurants (December 2000)

Restaurant	December Sales (£)
Oxford	256,185
Leicester	168,982
Derby	133,785
Burton	81,422
Wolverhampton	78,152
Bromsgrove	48,105
Milton Keynes	296,963
Colchester	109,976
Luton	51,434
Total	£1,225,004

Table 8.3 Employees by Job Category and Gender (December 2000)

Job Category	Males	Females
Area Manager	2	
Restaurant Manager	8	2
First Assistant	10	3
Second Assistant	12	8
Supervisor	10	24
Operative	51	361
Totals	93	398

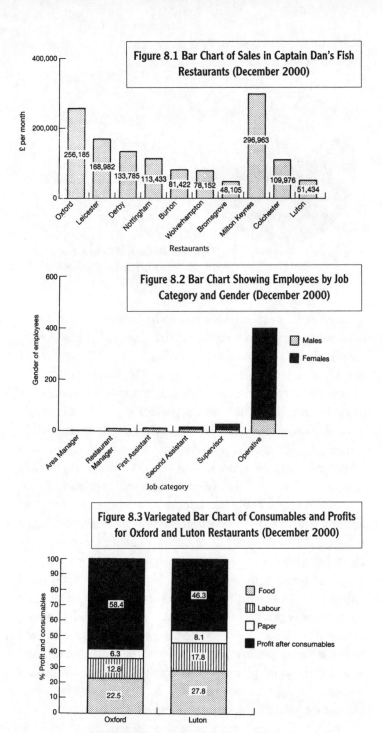

Figure 8.1 Bar Chart of Sales in Captain Dan's Fish Restaurants (December 2000)

£ per month

Oxford 256,185
Leicester 168,982
Derby 133,785
Nottingham 113,433
Burton 81,422
Wolverhampton 78,152
Bromsgrove 48,105
Milton Keynes 296,963
Colchester 109,976
Luton 51,434

Restaurants

Figure 8.2 Bar Chart Showing Employees by Job Category and Gender (December 2000)

Gender of employees

Males
Females

Area Manager, Restaurant Manager, First Assistant, Second Assistant, Supervisor, Operative

Job category

Figure 8.3 Variegated Bar Chart of Consumables and Profits for Oxford and Luton Restaurants (December 2000)

% Profit and consumables

Food
Labour
Paper
Profit after consumables

Oxford: 58.4, 6.3, 12.8, 22.5
Luton: 46.3, 8.1, 17.8, 27.8

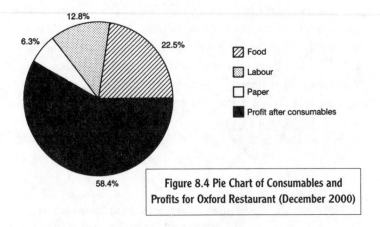

Figure 8.4 Pie Chart of Consumables and Profits for Oxford Restaurant (December 2000)

If more than one quality needs to be compared against each category a component (or variegated) bar chart can be useful. Here the benefit is a visual comparison of data within each category, as well as comparisons between categories. This can be most useful where categories are of different sizes. It is possible to visualize the different proportions within the categories. Figure 8.2 is an example of a component bar chart where there are two categories to compare, in this case the proportion of males and females in each job category. The chart dramatically shows how the gender mix changes as job categories move from managerial to operative levels.

Complete sets of data can be included in a variegated bar chart and this can allow the comparison of one or more sets of categories. Figure 8.3 is an example of a more complex component bar chart. In this case it compares two categories using percentage to even out the variations in the categories. A numerical scale could also be used. An alternative way of showing how proportions make up a whole is through the pie chart. Here the whole data are regarded as 360 degrees and the categories are converted into 'slices of the whole'. The larger the slice, the larger the category as a proportion of the whole. Pie charts can present difficulties unless used with a computer, because it is hard to manually convert the relative proportions to degrees of the circle.

12 STEPS TO STUDY SUCCESS

The pie chart can be a very effective means of representing proportions and relationships within data. However, they need to be used selectively because there are some important weaknesses. For example, if there are more than ten slices or slices are so small as to make them almost invisible, the visual impact may be lost. Also pie charts are less effective at comparing two sets of data, as done in Figure 8.3. Figure 8.4 is an example of a pie chart based on information provided for the Oxford restaurant in Figure 8.3.

Quantitative Data

A list of the value of sales transactions at a cash desk over a one-hour period is shown in Table 8.4. Each number in the list is referred to as a value of the variable, in this case money values. The list in this form is known as 'raw data'. Whilst raw data are most accurate because they represent the actual results, the data need organizing to give them some meaning and sense for those who wish to use them as an information source and for decision-making. The data have to be sorted to identify patterns and the formation of trends.

The tabulation of quantitative data

As was shown earlier, the tabulation of qualitative data starts with the identification of categories. With quantitative data the values occur in the same scale of measurement, in this case money. Tabulation of this sort of data starts with the division of the scale of values into sections or classes.

The lowest figure in Table 8.4 is 85 pence and the highest is £5.75. The set of classes should cover the range between these two classes in such a way that they do not overlap and there are no gaps. In other words the classification should be set up in such a way that each value can be located in a class without confusion or judgement.

Table 8.4 Value of Consecutive Transactions Between 10 and 11 a.m. on Monday 4th December 2000 (Oxford)

£0.85	£1.67	£2.29	£3.58
£4.46	£5.10	£0.97	£1.25
£1.37	£2.80	£2.89	£2.50
£3.45	£3.56	£3.46	£2.67
£0.97	£5.50	£2.75	£3.50
£3.50	£1.80	£1.80	£4.75
£5.75	£4.65	£0.85	£2.89
£3.80	£4.25	£5.35	£0.97
£1.80	£1.75	£1.89	£2.28
£4.75	£4.75	£1.90	£5.50
£1.70	£1.40	£2.80	£2.76
£2.75	£2.75	£2.50	£2.89
£3.80	£3.75		

One way of classifying the data in Table 8.4 is given opposite in Table 8.5. This is not the only way of classifying the data. To some extent this is a judgement which has to be made about the data and the use to which they are to be put. The judgement rests on the tension between the raw data, which is what actually happened, and creating classifications which give the data meaning and make the information usable. In the example under investigation, an alternative method could work on 50 pence categories which would have the effect of increasing the number of classes. The guideline to bear in mind is that there would normally be between 5 and 15 classes, and the number of classes should approximately match the square root of the number of values (in this case roughly seven). Where possible, class sizes should be even and it is usually easier to deal with class intervals of 5, 10 or multiples of 10.

Once the list of classes has been established, the number of values in each class is counted and noted. The table that results is

Table 8.5 Spend Values Between 10 and 11 a.m. on Monday 4 December 2000 (Oxford)

Transaction Values	Frequency
Under £1	5
£1.00 – 1.99	11
£2.00 – 2.99	14
£3.00 – 3.99	9
£4.00 – 4.99	6
£5.00 – 5.99	5
Total	

Table 8.6 Customer Party Size Entering the Restaurant between 10 and 11 a.m. on Monday 4 December 2000 (Oxford)

1	2	1	4	2	1	2	3	4	5
1	2	2	2	1	1	1	3	4	1
2	2	3	3	4	4	1	1	1	1
1	3	4	1	1	2	2	1	1	2

Table 8.7 Frequency Distribution of Customer Party Size Entering the Restaurant between 10 and 11 a.m. on Monday 4 December 2000 (Oxford)

Number in Party	Frequency
1	20
2	15
3	8
4	6
5	1
Total	50

a grouped frequency distribution. It is grouped because the values are sorted or grouped into classes, frequency because the table shows how many values occur in each class, and distribution because it shows how the values are scattered or 'distributed' across the range. Table 8.5 is an example of a grouped frequency distribution.

If a set of data consists of a series of frequently recurring values it may not be necessary to create a set of classes. Each value becomes a class. An example of this is given in Tables 8.6 and 8.7. Here the data refer to the number of customers entering a restaurant as a single party in a given period. As the data are not grouped into classes, Table 8.7 is now presented as a frequency distribution.

The presentation of quantitative data

Tabulated data can be presented in a number of forms; the most common is known as a histogram. Each class of data (or value if it is in the form outlined in Table 8.4) is depicted by a block whose area is in proportion to the frequency of values in the class. Figure 8.5 is a histogram of the distribution of the data in Table 8.5. The scale on the vertical axis must start at zero, because of the importance of the relative size of each block. This is not necessarily the case with the horizontal axis, although presentation is improved if it starts one class before the first class in the grouped frequency distribution. Only the beginning of each class is plotted on the horizontal axis.

On occasion it is useful to track trends over a period of time. This is known as time series data. Table 8.8 provides details of the annual sales of Captain Dan's Fish Restaurants between 1993 and 1999.

The data from Table 8.8 are plotted in the form of a line graph in Figure 8.6. In these cases time is always plotted along the horizontal axis so that reading from left to right the progression can be followed. The vertical scale should start at zero. Sometimes

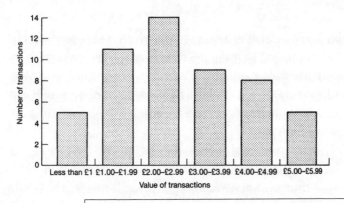

Figure 8.5 Histogram of Transactions Values Between
10 and 11 a.m. on Monday 4 December 2000 (Oxford)

Table 8.8 Annual Sales Revenue for Captain Dan's Fish Restaurants
(1993–1999)

Year	Sales revenue
1993	£2,500,000
1994	£4,700,000
1995	£6,200,000
1996	£7,500,000
1997	£6,750,000
1998	£10,200,000
1999	£14,700,000

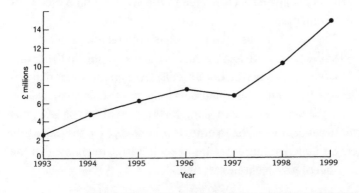

Figure 8.6 Line Graph Showing Annual Sales (1993-1999)

a time series consists of large numbers which change only slightly, and it is tempting to make the change appear more dramatic by starting the scale above zero. This is a device frequently used by popular newspapers, but which should be avoided because it can create a false impression. Figure 8.6 avoids this by converting the scale to £ millions.

The comparison of one set of variables with another can be useful. In effect a time series involves a comparison of this sort because time is a variable. In other cases, it may be that some other factor needs to be compared and this reveals more about the trend. In Table 8.9 the annual sales are compared with the number of restaurants open within the group. This results in a *bivariate analysis* and the first stage is the construction of a *scattergram*.

Each point in the diagram represents a pair of associated values, one value of each variable. In Figure 8.7 the level of annual sales is compared with number of restaurants open in the group. Visually the scattergram produces a pattern which establishes the correlation between these two variables. The more tightly the points are clustered round an imaginary line running upwards from left to right, the more closely the two variables appear to be related. The more dispersed the cluster of points, the less strongly the two variables are correlated. In some cases there may be an inverse relationship, that is, the two variables are correlated but in a negative way. For example, the growth in sales of video recorders is inversely correlated to the average number of visits to the cinema.

Figure 8.7 can be used to establish the relationship between sales revenue growth and the number of restaurants in the group. Here the number of restaurants is displayed on the horizontal axis because the number of restaurants is the independent variable and sales revenue is measured along the horizontal axis because it is the dependent variable. In other words, changes in the independent variable (restaurants) are likely to result in changes in the dependent variable (sales revenue).

Table 8.9 Annual Sales Revenue Compared With Restaurants (1993-1999)

Year	Sales Revenue	Restaurants
1993	£2,500,000	1
1994	£4,700,000	2
1995	£6,200,000	4
1996	£7,500,000	5
1997	£6,750,000	5
1998	£10,200,000	7
1999	£14,700,000	10

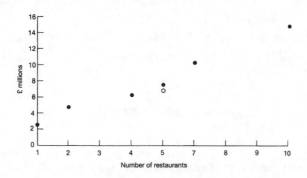

Figure 8.7 Scattergram of Annual Sales Revenue
and Restaurants (1993–1999)

Numerical presentation of quantitative data

In many cases, the use of some basic statistical measures as a
means of communicating information about a set of data can be
helpful and supportive of your written report. Thus the use of
some basic arithmetic techniques in the form of percentages,
ratios and index numbers, or some measures of dispersion in the
form of averages and measures of range can be usefully employed
as tools of presentation in written documents such as reports.

Some basic arithmetic techniques

A number of techniques are available to convert data into forms which allow comparison with non-similar data, or reveal proportions or trends within data. These are mostly simple arithmetic calculations which change the raw figures to some standard form. The most commonly employed of these uses a base of 100, hence the term percentage.

The variegated bar chart in Figure 8.3 uses percentages as a means of both showing controllable costs and profits as proportions of total revenue within each restaurant, and allowing comparison between restaurants. Thus, in the example, the component cost structure can be compared even though the monthly sales in Oxford are five times greater than those in Luton.

The formula involves the creation of a fraction which is then converted to a percentage through multiplication of the fraction by 100.

Formula: $\dfrac{\textbf{Proportion}}{\textbf{Base}} \times \textbf{100} = \textbf{per cent}$

What percentage of total sales is the labour cost in the Oxford restaurant?

Labour costs = £32,791
Sales   = £256,185

$$\frac{32,791}{256,185} \times 100 = 17.8\%$$

Whilst percentages are useful, caution should be exercised in their use. A frequent mistake made by students is to use them in the wrong situations. For example, where the base figure is low, changes in a small number result in dramatic shifts in the percentage.

A second technique establishes ratios between data by showing how one item compares with another. Ratios allow a constant relationship to be applied to different base figures. Ratios are calculated by establishing a fraction, which is then simplified to a proportional relationship. For example, the kitchen profit method of costing in some traditional restaurants often assumes a permanent ratio between food material costs and the selling price of 1:2.5. Hence a dish with food costs of £2 would be priced on the menu at £5.00.

Ratio 1:2.5
Food costs £2 × 2.5 = £5.00 selling price

A third technique uses index numbers by converting data back to some common base figure (usually 1, 10 or 100) and then comparing new data against the base figure. This is frequently used in government statistical analysis, say in price inflation comparisons, where today's prices are compared with some base year, say 1960.

In other situations index numbers are useful because trends within different sets of data can be compared. For example, in the above example, an index number can be used to establish the sales revenue in 1999 compared with 1993. Here the base year is 1993 (sales £2,500,000) and this will be given the value of 100. The year to be compared will be 1999 (sales £14,700,000). The calculation is similar to that for percentages, though the base year is always the same.

Formula: $\dfrac{\text{Comparator}}{\text{Base}} \times 100 = \text{Index}$

$$\frac{14,700,000}{2,500,000} \times 100 = 588$$

Thus in this example, the figures show that sales in 1999 were 588 compared to the base year (100) in 1993. This might be helpful when comparing performance with some external trend, say in the growth of the market or a competitor, or comparing trends within the organization, say by comparing sales growth with labour cost growth.

Measures of location

The common name for measures of location is averages. An average is a simple and effective way of communicating much information in a single figure.

The average annual turnover of these restaurants is £1.4 million. The average annual turnover for their major competitor is £900,000.

The average number of transactions per hour in the Oxford restaurant was 15.1. In the Luton restaurant the average number of transactions was 6.8 per hour.

In both cases, a single figure has been used to create a clear impression of average value sales revenue in one case and transactions in the other. Representing sets of figures in this way is an essential element in effectively communicating quantitative data.

The use of the average is not without problems. In the first place the term 'average' can be used to describe different terms; the mean, median and mode. Each of these terms is described as a 'measure of location' because each identifies a point around which a set of numerical values are arranged or located. An alternative term is the 'measure of central tendency' which also gives the impression of a numerical centre to a set of values.

The mean

When most people talk about the average they usually mean the arithmetic mean. It is arrived at by adding up a set of values and then dividing it by the number of values.

Example: 3, 4, 7, 10

$$\text{The mean} \quad (x) = \frac{(3 + 4 + 7 + 10)}{4} = 6$$

In the information provided in Table 8.6, 103 people visited the restaurant within the period studied and made 50 transactions. What was the average (mean) number of people in each transaction?

$$\frac{103}{50} = 2.06$$

When considering the arithmetic mean it is necessary to recognize that this measure has both strengths and weaknesses. It is quite helpful in that it is easily understood and easy to calculate. It also includes all values in the calculation, and is therefore thought to be a true representation of the set of values. The major weakness of this measure is that it can easily be distorted by high or low values. The second problem is that it may produce values which are not feasible for the value to take. For example, in the figures above the mean party size is 2.06 people.

The median

The median provides the 'middle value' in a set of values. In other words it represents the mid-point in the spread of values and can take out distortions produced by either high or low values. To calculate the median, the data must be first arranged in an array. That is, arranged in order of magnitude from lowest to the highest value. The mid-point is then easily identified.

Example: array 3, 4, 5, 7, 10

The median is 5

A slight complication arises if there is an even number of values. In such cases the median is the mean of the middle pair of values.

Example: 7, 4, 10, 3, 5, 9

Array: 3, 4, 5, 7, 9, 10

$$\text{Median} = \frac{(5+7)}{2} = 6$$

In the example created earlier in Table 8.7, the median value of numbers of persons per transaction is 2, because the middle point between the 25th and 26th point in the array is in the class of values for two-person transactions.

The median is simple to understand, it is not distorted by unusually high or low values, and it produces a feasible value. The key problem is that it will not be featured in further statistical analysis, because it is not calculated from the full set of real values.

Finally, the principle of the median can be used to split a set of values through the use of quartiles or deciles. In the first case the technique is used to find the value of the 'upper quartile', the top quarter of the values, or the 'lower quartile', the lower quarter of the values. In the second case the values are split up into tenths. In both these cases these techniques are useful in identifying the degree of distortion produced by sets of values which are distorted at the extremes. For example, they are frequently used to identify the uneven spread of income distribution in Britain.

The mode

The mode establishes the value which occurs most frequently within a set. In the examples given in Tables 8.6 and 8.7, the modal value is 1 because 20 of the 50 transactions were found to include one person, whilst only 15 transactions included two people, etc.

The key advantages are that the mode is easy to understand, it is not distorted by unusual values and will always be based on a feasible value. The key disadvantage is that, like the median, it cannot be used for further analysis because it cannot be used to reflect the true value of the set.

The Presentation of Qualitative and Quantitative Data

Both qualitative and quantitative data are useful in supporting and reinforcing the key themes in the analysis, problem solving and in the reporting of findings of an investigation. A presentation, whether it be verbal or written, is likely to be improved by the use of some of the techniques outlined in this step. It is important to remember, however, that these are tools to assist in developing and communicating understanding. They are essentially about communication and it is necessary to think carefully about the techniques which best aid understanding and further communication.

Revision and Review

✓ Effective presentations, written or verbal, will be strengthened by the presentation of qualitative and quantitative data.

✓ Each technique is valuable for communicating a particular view or perception of the data, and careful consideration needs to be given to the selection of appropriate techniques.

✓ There are rules about the professional presentation of tables and figures and these must be applied.

✓ Remember that these techniques are primarily needed to assist understanding and they should be located in the text, close to where they are to be discussed.

Essays and Reports

In this step you will consider:

✓ *Planning and preparation of written assignments*

✓ *How to write an academic essay*

✓ *How to prepare a report*

✓ *Basic rules of grammar*

✓ *Some special features of academic reports*

The Importance of Written Work

Success on most courses will very largely depend on the quality of the written material, which you submit. Clearly, presentations and other assessed activities will play some part, but the major weighting of the course grading will be related to various written outputs in the form of essays, reports and the dissertation, and in examinations.

Whilst general principles about the approach to writing can be applied to all of these media, each has specific requirements in the conventions which apply to essay writing, report/dissertation writing and examinations. It is the purpose of this step to focus specifically on the requirements of essays and reports. Step 11 looks at the specific requirements of examinations.

The major differences between essays and reports are related to the purpose, presentation, format and structure, and style of the two documents. Common approaches relate to the planning process, the flow and organization of material, and the use of quotations and references. These common issues will be dealt with first and then we shall examine the specific requirements of essays and reports.

Common Ground

Clearly one of the major differences between essays and reports is that their traditions and roles are set in different contexts. The writing of essays is largely an activity restricted to the academic world, whereas the report owes its origins to the world of work. However, within the context of your course both perform summative and formative functions. In other words, they assist both students and lecturers in summing up what the student understands about a particular topic; and are an important learning device in themselves.

Understanding the task

Analysing the question and clearly identifying what is required to complete the task is crucial. It may sound obvious, but one of the most common mistakes made by students is a failure to answer the question set. In the case of reports it may be that terms of reference are supplied and these should form the basis for your report. In some cases you may be asked to define terms of reference yourself.

Your analysis of the task should raise a series of questions, which your essay/report will attempt to answer.

Collecting material

Your analytical questions will to a large extent direct your information-gathering exercise. They should form a plan of the sorts of issues you wish to follow up.

Clearly, the sources of information may well be different for both reports and essays. These sources of information are discussed in Step 7.

Your research and further reading may well raise new questions or lead you to amend those you have written.

Early start

You need time to mull over and amend your ideas. Often other influences say in casual conversation or in another study area, will suggest new avenues to follow up.

Keep a notebook

A small notebook in which to jot down ideas is good practice. This can prove invaluable in recording ideas and experiences as they occur and spark ideas relevant to your task.

Secondary sources of information

In most cases you will be gathering information from books, periodicals, academic journals, newspapers, the internet etc.

→ *Be selective* in your reading.

→ *Note down* the key points of each article/chapter.

→ *Arrange* the notes in relation to the questions you have identified.

→ *Ensure* that possible useful references or *quotations are identified* and sourced as you go through the readings. There is nothing more frustrating or time-wasting than searching for that reference you vaguely remember exists somewhere.

→ *Apart* from quotations it is a good idea to write notes in *your own words*. One of the distinguishing features of a poor essay is the inclusion of large chunks of material copied from books and passed off as the student's own words. Taken to extremes this can raise issues of plagiarism.

The importance of planning

A common weakness of much written material seen by lecturers is that it lacks structure or is over-balanced in one aspect or another. By and large this is caused by a failure to plan.

✦ Write a brief outline of what you want the piece to say – in other words, what is the 'big idea' behind your essay or report? Fifty to 100 words will do.

✦ Refer to the outline regularly. It keeps you on the right track and prevents over-writing or under-writing key sections.

+ Produce a detailed plan of the structure. This will be different for essays and reports; both will include an introduction and a conclusion, with the main body of topics or sections in the middle.

+ Bearing in mind the overall length being aimed at, write a target number of words for each section. A 2000-word essay with three major sections and eight sub-sections might look like Table 9.1.

Table 9.1 Examples of an Essay Word Plan

Introduction			250 words
Theme I			500
	(i)	100	
	(ii)	200	
	(iii)	200	
Theme II			600
	(i)	300	
	(ii)	300	
Theme III			400
	(i)	100	
	(ii)	200	
	(iii)	100	
Conclusion			250
		Total	2000 words

Some students prefer to write the introduction first, others prefer to write it after the main body of work has been written. By using a well-organized plan, you should be able to write the various sections out of sequence.

Sequencing the material

You will find that both the essays and the reports, which you have to prepare in your course, will require different approaches to sequencing the material, depending on the task given. In the main, most essays will tend to be 'argumentative' whilst reports will tend to be 'analytical'. However, this is not always the case. Figure 9.1 highlights two models, which could be followed if you were writing an essay with the following title.

> **'Money is the only motivator for those who work in the hospitality industry.' Discuss this statement in the light of motivation theory.**

In the example in Figure 9.1, Sequence A is structured round an exposition of the theories, or types of theories, which might be covered in answer to the question. This is a structure frequently applied by students. Whilst it can result in a reasonable essay, more often than not it results in an essay, which is descriptive, because the structure itself will lead the writer to describe one theory after another.

Sequence A may be appropriate to a report, though it will depend on the nature of the report brief.

Sequence B, on the other hand, attempts to establish a framework of themes against which to discuss and compare each set of theories. The result is more likely to be argumentative, because it encourages contrasting and comparing of the different theories. It will also be more analytical, because it encourages a discussion that analyses theories against common themes.

The nature of the exercise, the level of the course, the subject matter and the expectations of lecturers will determine the appropriate structure, but it is a good idea to spend some time thinking about these issues.

Style

Keep your style straightforward and uncomplicated. Write short sentences, avoid slang or jargon. Often it is a good idea to try and edit down that which you have written. It makes a much more punchy read.

◆ *Avoid unsubstantiated assertions; try to justify what you say.*

◆ *Keep your style objective.*

Dealing with arguments

Writing for the arts and social sciences topics rarely involves situations where there is a consensus of views held by different theorists. In most cases there are different views, some with which you agree and others with which you disagree. In most cases your written output will be expected to reflect this range of views and theories.

◆ *Don't be afraid to take sides, but you must deal effectively with the full range of arguments, particularly with those of the opposing view.*

◆ *A feature of the best work is that it expresses the writer's views in a way that deals with all arguments and views.*

Sequence A

Theories	People
Money is the motivator *Taylor*	Are all jobholders in the same position? Managers, skilled workers, semi-skilled, unskilled?
Content Theories. *Maslow, Herzberg, MacGregor*, etc.	Are all jobholders in the same position? Managers, skilled workers, semi-skilled, unskilled?
Process Theories *Expectancy, Equity*	Are all jobholders in the same position? Managers, skilled workers, semi-skilled, unskilled?

Sequence B

Theories	Themes	People

Taylor
Content Theories
  Maslow, Herzberg,
  MacGregor, etc.
Process Theories
  Expectancy, Equity
	What they say about money as a motivator	Are all jobholders in the same position?
		Managers, skilled workers, semi-skilled, unskilled?

Taylor
Content Theories
  Maslow, Herzberg,
  MacGregor, etc.
Process Theories
  Expectancy, Equity
	What they say about job satisfaction	Are all jobholders in the same position?
		Managers, skilled workers, semi-skilled, unskilled?

Taylor
Content Theories
  Maslow, Herzberg,
  MacGregor, etc.
Process Theories
  Expectancy, Equity
	What they say about individual differences	Are all jobholders in the same position?
		Managers, skilled workers, semi-skilled, unskilled?

Figure 9.1 Two Methods of Sequencing Written Material

Presentation

It is expected that all work is well presented and reflects a professional standard. Whilst you will not be penalized for hand-written work, in most cases it is a good idea to present your work in a typed or word-processed form. If you do have to hand-write your work then ensure it is neat and legible, and allow plenty of space.

Remember, lecturers are human and are likely to view more favourably work which is easy to read and demonstrates quickly what the student knows.

Again one of the common features of a good essay or academic report is the appropriate use of references and quotations. In both cases these will add scholarly weight to your work, but must be properly dealt with, see Step 12 *The Dissertation*

References are vital in that they indicate your source for a particular statement or view. The text is written in your own words, expressing the view or concept intended, but should show the journal or book from whence they came.

Roddick (1988) makes the point that economic recovery in the OECD countries helped to attract funds with which to finance their own recovery.

Quotations are a direct quote, word for word, from some other source – book, magazine, journal article, etc. The key point is that this must be treated in the following way if the quotation is more than one line of words. First it must be indented from the text. There should be a space between it and the text – preceding and following. The quotation should be followed by the author's name, year of publication and page number.

'The major economic recovery of major western powers from 1977 onwards helped to change this picture, sucking funds back

into the OECD countries to pay for newly profitable home-based activities.'

(J. Roddick, 1988, p. 35)

In both cases, the Reference section at the end of your work should include a list of the texts to which you have referred or from which you have taken a quotation. There are several systems for doing this; the following is based on the 'Harvard System'. The list is arranged alphabetically according to the authors' surnames and years of publication. Thus the above would appear as follows:

Roddick, J. (1988) *The Dance of Millions*. Latin American Bureau: London.

Revision and proof reading

Once you have written your assignment, it is a good idea to set it aside for a short period and then review it critically. Mistakes, clumsy language and errors in structure may be easier to detect at this stage. In some cases it is advisable to get another person to check it over for you.

This process requires that you allow plenty of time between completing this first draft and the deadline for handing in the work. Unfortunately, many students submit work that has not been through this process. Grades are thus lower than they might be.

Writing Essays

For many students on arts and social science programmes (including business and management), the academic essay probably presents the most wide-reaching change in style from prior study. Even those who have written essays on earlier courses may yet have something to learn about the expectations of a formal academic essay.

You must think carefully about these issues and approach the essay task with the following points in mind.

The majority of suggestions made above apply to your approach to essay writing. In other words, you must think carefully about the essay title and the questions it raises; prepare by gathering the information and doing the background reading. You must carefully plan the structure and sequencing of the essay. You must adopt the correct style, deal with the range of arguments and present the document in a professional manner. It must contain good use of references and quotations.

Essays will use different terms in the question. Each term has a meaning that reveals how the question should be answered. The following list is an example of some words that you might come across. These should be considered for both course work essays and for the essays you may be given under examination conditions. Examination practice is discussed more fully in Step 11.

Some words commonly used in essay questions and their meanings

Account for	Give reasons for, explain, clarify.
Analyse	Examine critically or in detail. Break down into component parts.
Assess	Consider the value of; weigh up (see evaluate).
Compare	Explore similarities and differences between the items mentioned in the question (theories, ideologies, etc.).
Contrast	Look for the differences between the items mentioned.
Compare and contrast	Explore the similarities and differences between items. Usually the best approach is to examine a common framework of analysis so as to be able to show where they are similar and where different.

Criticize	Through a discussion of the evidence or arguments supporting a theory or opinion; make a judgement about its merit.
Define	State the meaning of a word or phrase.
Describe	Give a detailed account of something.
Discuss	Explain and then give different views about, or implications of the item.
Distinguish	Look for differences between (also covers differentiate between).
Evaluate	Determine the worth, value or validity of something through an examination of the supporting arguments or theories.
Examine the argument	Critically explore this line of thinking, argument, opinion, etc.
Explain	Give details about how and why.
Illustrate	Make clear and explicit; often requires the use of examples.

An inspection of past question papers or essay questions will help you to get a feel for the types of questions which tutors like to ask and the style of answers required.

Features of a good essay

→ It addresses the question asked. This means the answer must be applied to the question asked, and not merely everything you know about the topic.

→ It deals with all the key points and a range of arguments or viewpoints. A frequent weakness in student essays is that they reflect limited sources of material, and hence contain only a narrow spectrum of views.

→ It is written in an objective style that avoids unsubstantiated assertions. It is free of spelling and grammatical errors. It creates a professional impression.

→ It shows evidence of wide reading. This relates to the point made above, but is important because your essay needs to show that you have read widely, through the use of references and quotations, and range of arguments covered.

→ It uses both references and quotations in an appropriate manner. References must be widely used to support the substance of your essay. Quotations must be used sparingly. They should be short and carefully selected.

→ It is written in the student's own words and has a sense of his or her own 'voice'. A frequent weakness is that essays reflect material from books. Apart from issues to do with plagiarism, this makes the essay disjointed and clumsy in style.

→ It is analytical in structure and questioning in approach.

→ It has a carefully crafted introduction, i.e. one that raises the key issues or questions, and identifies the approach to be taken by the writer.

→ The main development of the essay follows a logical flow and is balanced. The structure of the main body of the essay is based on an analytical approach and is well planned so that themes are balanced in a manner appropriate to the topic. It is within the word limit.

→ It concludes with a well-crafted conclusion. This highlights the points raised and conclusions made in the essay.

→ It is neat and well presented, preferably typed, on single sides of A4.

→ It will contain a reference section and bibliography.

There may well be variations amongst different module tutors, or course teams about the precise expectations of student essays. Different subjects in the arts and social sciences do require different approaches, but attention does need to be paid to these issues before you start to plan and prepare your essay. Many students fail to maximize their grades because they fail to address the issue of essay expectations early enough in the course.

Reports

Again many of the points made in the early part of this step apply to the report format. However, this has a formal structure that will be outlined in detail below. Clearly, short reports will not include all the sections suggested, though they will contain most.

Lecturers will be assessing the professionalism of your work. To be successful it must be business-like and worthy of being used in a 'real-life' situation. The report is a business document; it is a device for aiding speedy communication of important issues.

Contents: all but the shortest of reports should contain a contents page listing all main section headings together with the page numbers on which they are to be found.

Summary: a brief summary should sum up the main contents, findings, conclusions and recommendations in the report. The purpose of this section is to give a busy person a quick overview of the report's contents. Usually one side of A4 is sufficient, so the bywords are brevity and clarity. In many industrial situations, this will come before the contents page.

Introduction: this is the introduction to the main part of the report. It sets the scene for the reader. It performs a valuable communicative role, i.e. it tells the reader what is coming up. It outlines the key issues and concerns. Why is the report necessary? It also tells the reader how these issues will be dealt with. It should also interest the reader, make him/her want to read more.

Research methods/background: depending on the nature of the report, it may be necessary to set the report in context, give general background or history. Although part of the introductory process, this information is not included in the introduction.

In the cases of other reports, it will be necessary to describe the method by which the writer has gathered information and conducted the investigation. For example, where did the investigation take place, how was the information gathered and analysed, etc.?

For some reports, both Background and Research Methods will be needed.

Problem description, analysis and possible solutions: again the way you develop the main body of the report will depend on the brief and scope of the report.

It should contain headed sections dealing with the main topics being discussed. It should follow a logical sequence, moving from the descriptive to the analytical. It must contain all the information needed to justify the conclusions and recommendations to follow.

The selection of appropriate information is crucial here. The rule of thumb is that where information is important to aid understanding it should be included.

Figures and tables: most reports will need to include various non-verbal forms of communication. These should be included in the text to aid communication. In both cases, figures (diagrams, graphs, charts) or tables (rows and columns of numbers and/or text), must be properly labelled, neatly presented and sourced.

These should be laid out and sequenced along the lines given in Step 8. More detailed data may be included in the appendix.

Conclusions: this section highlights the findings of the report. It will pick up the themes outlined in the introduction and show what has been established.

Recommendations: depending on the assignment being set, this section will make specific recommendations for future action. These will always lead from the main body of the report.

Appendices: where appropriate this will provide further background information that may be useful to the interested reader. For example, where the report deals with the results of a questionnaire survey, it may be helpful to include a copy of the questionnaire in the Appendix.

A common error is for students to put all figures and tables in the Appendix. Where these aid understanding, they should be put in the main body of the report.

Bibliography: of books, articles, or texts that have been used, as source material must be included with all reports.

Many courses will require students to submit an academic report or dissertation. In some respects the academic report/dissertation reflects several of the features of both academic essays and reports. This subject is dealt with more fully in Step 12 *The Dissertation*.

Grammar

An area where students consistently fall down is in their poor use of grammar. Excellent books have been written on the subject and it is not the intention to replicate the detail of those volumes here. We will just examine areas of particular weakness, where mistakes are commonly made.

Tense, Number and People

You should try and ensure that there is consistency between tense, number and person, for example

'Simply practising ten minutes a day helped Michael make fewer mistakes, when he tries to pass the ball.'

OK so you spotted that one. The author is using both the *present* tense (when he tries) along with the *past tense* (practising) in the same sentence. It could have read:

'Simply practising ten minutes a day helped Michael make fewer mistakes, when he tried to pass the ball.'

Or

'Simply practising ten minutes a day helps Michael make fewer mistakes, when he tries to pass the ball.'

Now look at this sentence and see what is wrong.

'A professional table tennis player is aware of their spatial skills.'

This one is a little harder and subtler, but it could have read either

'Professional table tennis players are aware of their spatial skills.'

Or

'A professional table tennis player is aware of his or her spatial skills.'

Linking Sentences to form Paragraphs

Generally students write sentences that are far *too long* and contain *more than one point* often with several points they *forget to punctuate* and sometimes have just *one sentence to make up a paragraph*.

Ideally, each *sentence* should describe or discuss just *one point*. A paragraph should be made up of several linked sentences covering a *single topic*. Linking words are called *conjunctions*. *First of all, after this, then, secondly* and *finally* are used to link sentences and also phrases within sentences. These words fulfil several purposes, they are to:

◆ **Summarize**, for example: it has been argued; the proceeding pages indicate; in consequence; in conclusion.

◆ **Provide an opposing or opposite view**: conversely; on the other hand; an alternative view is held by; in contrast.

◆ **Amplify an argument** or add to information already discussed: furthermore; in addition to; moreover; besides.

◆ **Flag up the order** of presentation, or discussions: Firstly; secondly; then; prior to; in conclusion.

Spelling
Most work is now word-processed and there is an automatic spell checker with these. It is a good discipline to spell check the final draft before printing. It is also useful to regularly check words that you are unsure of in a dictionary.

Capital Letters
All sentences begin with a capital letter, as do all place and personal names. Sometimes capitals are used in titles, or headings at the beginning of each word, as in the above example.

Homophones
These are words that sound the same and are spelt differently. This is an area where students often get into difficulty. Overleaf is a list of some homophones.

Main	Mane	
Sail	Sale	
Mail	Male	
There	Their	They're
Pail	Pale	
Whether	Weather	
Principle	Principal	
Practice	Practise	
Two	To	Too
Horse	Hoarse	
Led	Lead	
Assent	Ascent	
Desert	Dessert	
Stationary	Stationery	
Sell	Cell	

Punctuation

The three main tools of punctuation are the comma, full stop and the apostrophe; all have specific rules as to their use. There are other punctuation marks that can be used within the text, for example the colon, semi-colon and the hyphen. These do not have such common usage and their description is beyond the scope of this book.

Comma: Generally commas are used to make small stretches within longer sentences. They tend to be used where you would pause if reading aloud to make the passage make sense. Another use of the comma is when describing lists. There are only exceptional circumstances where commas are used directly either side of the word 'and'.

Full stop: These are usually used to signal the end of a sentence, although sentences may also end with either a question mark (?) or an exclamation mark (!). Another use of a full stop is where a word has been abbreviated, generally where there is convention for this. However the full stop is only used where the shortened word ends in a different letter. For example December is abbreviated to Dec. whereas Doctor is abbreviated to Dr with no full stop.

Apostrophe ('): There are three reasons for using the apostrophe. Firstly it can denote possession. Secondly it can be used where the word has been shortened and there are some letters missing. Finally it can be used to denote plural of either letters or numerals. For example: *'One must remember one's P's and Q's'*

> *Examples of the first case follow:*
>
> *The engineer's report was very damaging.*
>
> *The course leader's responsibilities included compiling a course report.*
>
> *The tribunal upheld the chef's claim for unfair dismissal.*

NOTE, if the noun is plural the apostrophe goes after the possessive noun. In the instance of example two above, if we were referring to course leaders collectively, the sentence would read:

The course leaders' responsibilities included compiling course reports.

Where letters are missing the apostrophe goes into the space, often the word needing the apostrophe derives from the amalgamation of two words, for example:

There's (there is), didn't (did not), hasn't (has not), couldn't (could not), I'm (I am), we're (we are).

Colloquialisms

Certain phrases and words are often used when we speak, that would be inappropriate within academic writing. Some examples, submitted by students, follow:

'**At the end of the day**, the company has improved **no end** compared with the previous year's figures. They really have **got their act together**.'

'To motivate the work force you've got to let them **have a bit of a crack** to relieve pressure, as long as it doesn't damage company property.'

'It's true in this instance they have **dropped a bit of a clanger** and the staffing levels have to be looked at **with a sense of urgency**'

'To effect a **dramatic turnaround** the senior management have to take new proposed working practices **on board**.'

Can you mark any other grammatical errors in the four examples given?

Don't try and write as you speak, it is not acceptable in academic or any professional writing.

Revision and Review

✓ The successful completion of written essays, reports and dissertations is likely to be a key factor in the assessment on your course.

✓ There are many common features to the way you approach these tasks. Planning and time management are essential.

✓ Academic essays have particular features that you must understand and incorporate in your work. Chiefly, the need to include academic references is an essential element.

✓ An academic report or dissertation combines many features of both reports and essays. It needs to include a thorough review of the literature as well as a clear outline of the primary research that you have undertaken.

✓ Grammar is an area where many students fall down; do not write as you speak.

Making Presentations

In this step you will consider:

✓ *Your experiences of making presentations*

✓ *Some common difficulties in verbal presentations*

✓ *The characteristics of a good presentation*

✓ *How to overcome anxiety*

✓ *Visual aids and their effective use*

Most courses will expect you to make verbal presentations to fellow students and tutors. In some cases you will be participating in a group presentation; however, in most instances you will be assessed on your individual performance. It is essential therefore that you approach this activity with confidence and in a systematic manner.

Consider a recent presentation you have made. How did it go? What were the strengths and weaknesses of your performance? List these below.

Strengths	Weaknesses
1	1
2	2
3	3
4	4
5	5
6	6
7	7

Some Common Problems with Presentations

Problems encountered when making presentations can probably be simplified to three major problem areas:

- ✦ a lack of preparation

- ✦ anxiety

- ✦ an absence of or poor visual aids and support materials

Preparation

Poor preparation results in ill-timed presentations lacking in structure. They will often be pitched at a level inappropriate to the audience.

A speaker who is not well prepared will soon 'lose' the audience and this in turn will reduce confidence and create greater anxiety. As part of the planning process the speaker should:

→ Develop the aims and objectives of the presentation.

→ Consider the audience, their needs, background and prior knowledge of the topic.

→ Plan the key points to be made and their sequence. It is a good idea to limit the number of themes in your presentation – do not make the presentation over-complex.

→ Plan the presentation using keywords. Writing out the full text of a speech is a mistake. Invariably the delivery is boring.

→ Plan visual aids and handouts. Remember these should support the presentation, reinforcing key points and helping the audience to visualize what you are saying.

→ Structure the introduction to give an overview of what will be said.

→ Develop a strong conclusion. This should reinforce the key themes/points.

→ Rehearse the presentation using visual aids.

→ Check out the venue and equipment.

→ Consider dress and appearance so as to maximize authority.

→ Think success.

Anxiety

Anxiety is probably the most widespread cause of poor presentation performance amongst students. Whilst some anxiety is valuable because it gives an edge to the performance, too much anxiety is debilitating.

Practice in making presentations does help to reduce the anxiety, but there are also steps which you can take to keep it in manageable proportions.

→ **Be organized**. Good preparation and organization go a long way to reducing anxiety.

→ **Think success**. Visualize yourself in the room giving a successful presentation. Think of role models, people you have thought of as good presenters. Imagine you are them, copy what they did. It is a good idea to try and think of the things that could go wrong, and plan how you will deal with them.

→ **Practice**. Run through the presentation a couple of times using the visual aids. Make it as close to the final version as you can. Time it. Don't be afraid to chop out parts if it is too long. A common problem is over-production of material. People fear running out of things to say so they prepare too much and have to amend their presentation on the day. Try and get a colleague to witness your practice run, or try and video-tape it.

→ **Breathe deeply**. A few good deep breaths before you start speaking will help you to relax.

→ **Relax**. Tell yourself you are relaxed. Don't think of the audience as an audience, but as a single person in your sitting room or in the pub. Don't focus on your fear, but on the interesting things you have to say.

→ **Release tension**. Tension can make your body shake. A few simple isometric exercises, tensing and relaxing muscles, can help to release this.

→ **Move around**. Speakers who stay rigidly in one spot are likely to become tense. Moving your body helps it relax. Making gestures and moving across the speaking area can be a way of relaxing, although this needs to be carefully managed because the audience can find it distracting.

→ **Eye contact**. You will find this helps you relax because it brings you closer to the audience. You can imagine this as being just on a one-to-one basis. Also their eye contact with you is a good indicator of their interest.

Visual aids

All your presentations are likely to benefit from well-selected and well-presented visual aids.

→ Use visual aids for a purpose

✦ *to focus the audience's attention*

✦ *to reinforce your verbal message*

✦ *to stimulate interest*

✦ *to illustrate factors which are hard to visualize*

→ Avoid using visuals

✦ *just to impress your audience with very detailed information*

✦ *to avoid interacting with the audience*

- ◆ *to make your presentation over-complex*
- ◆ *to present simple ideas which can be stated verbally*

→ When constructing visual aids

- ◆ *use the KISS principle – keep it short and simple*
- ◆ *use only keywords or phrases*
- ◆ *ensure they are labelled for easy understanding*
- ◆ *select the form of chart or table which visualizes the points you are making*
- ◆ *don't overload the audience*
- ◆ *ensure they can be seen by all of the audience*

Remember

- ◆ *A picture is worth a thousand words.*
- ◆ *Engage the audience's right-hand side of the brain.*

Contrast and compare the visual aids in Figures 10.1 and 10.2. Which of these convey the key information with clarity? Which uses the right-hand side of the brain more effectively? Which are you most likely to remember if you are in the audience?

	Sales	PAC	Labour	Food	Paper
Unit 1	259,000	60.5	14.5	20.5	4.5
Unit 2	125,590	56.5	17.5	21.7	3.8
Unit 3	191,675	59.6	16.3	20.1	4.0
Unit 4	259,000	60.5	14.5	20.5	4.5
Unit 5	125,890	56.5	17.5	21.7	3.8
Unit 6	191,675	59.6	16.3	20.1	4.0
Unit 7	259,000	60.5	14.5	20.5	4.5
Unit 8	125,890	56.5	17.5	21.7	3.8
Unit 9	191,675	59.6	16.3	20.1	4.0

Many students do not use visual aids to support their presentations. Those who do not make visual aids frequently fail to consider the visual impact and the right-hand side of the brain. Visual aids should be visual and they should aid understanding. They should underpin the points being made in the talk. They should be visible from all parts of the room and should help the audience to understand what is being said. One of the most common mistakes is shown here – there is too much information on the OHP and the layout does not communicate effectively.

Figure 10.1 Examples of Unsuccessful Visual Aids

The Range of Unit performance

	Sales	PAC	Labour	Food	Paper
High	£259,000	60.5%	14.5%	20.5%	4.5%
Low	£125,890	56.5%	17.5%	21.7%	3.8%

Using visual aids to support presentations

- Use visual aids to support and enhance your presentation
- Consider the visual impact and the right side of the brain
- Visual aids should be visual and should aid understanding
- They should underpin the points being made in the talk
- They should be visible from all parts of the room

Figure 10.2 Examples of Successful Visual Aids

Making a Good Presentation

The characteristics of a good presentation are:

- ✦ Well prepared
- ✦ Appropriate material
- ✦ Interesting
- ✦ Concise
- ✦ Structured
- ✦ Well timed
- ✦ Good visual aids
- ✦ Supporting handouts

The characteristics of a good speaker are:

- ✦ Confidence
- ✦ Plenty of eye contact
- ✦ Good body language
- ✦ Speaking from notes, not reading
- ✦ Commanding attention
- ✦ Speaking with authority

Presentations to students, lectures and later in work situations give many people anxiety and stress. Much of this can be reduced by following the points listed above, and by practice. This is an activity which becomes easier the more you do it.

Revision and Review

✓ Many people have difficulties in making presentations, but with the correct approach, these can be overcome.

✓ Prepare for the presentation and make sure of what you have to say and to whom.

✓ Be positive and take steps to overcome your anxieties.

✓ Carefully prepare your visual aids to support your presentation.

✓ Make sure you practise the presentation and anticipate possible questions.

Examination Skills

In this step you will consider:

✓ *How to prepare for examinations*

✓ *How to organize revision*

✓ *Some common examination problems*

✓ *How to work in the examination*

Introduction

This section aims to give you guidance on the most effective way to approach the examinations which you will encounter in your course of study. It will deal with two broad themes which are essential for successful completion of examinations. A systematic approach to examination preparation and the planned use of your time in the examination hall will ensure that you are giving yourself the best chance of success.

Before We Start

Think about your most recent examination experience. What problems did you have? Did you do as well as you expected? What problems and difficulties did you encounter?

1.

2.

3.

4.

5.

6.

7.

About Examinations

Most courses of study in higher education will include some examinations in the package of assessments. The form and types of examinations may be many and varied and it is important to understand what is going to be expected of you in the examination situation. Here are some examples:

Unseen essay-style questions: this is a somewhat traditional style of examination which will require a paced response (making sure that you attempt all questions), and the correct level of answer. Typically, for courses in higher education, these will require more than knowledge and understanding; they may well expect you to be able to synthesize and evaluate information.

Unseen short answer questions: usually these are designed to test a breadth of knowledge and understanding, defining theory or terms.

Seen or unseen case studies: here the intention is to test your ability to apply information, theories and concepts. Again you will be expected to do much more than repeat what you know. This kind of paper requires application to the context in a realistic way.

Examination papers may well include more than one of these types of questions. They may include simulations, multiple-choice questions, or be based on computer exercises. The key point is that you must discover how you are to be examined and the type of paper which you will face.

Preparing for the Examination

The most effective preparation begins at the start of the unit or subject on which you will be examined. You will find examination preparation much easier if you have continued to revise and review your notes as the programme of lectures, seminars and tutorials progresses.

Often examination preparation is difficult because students have to re-learn material they once understood, but have now forgotten. It is a good idea to make a note of all the topics you have studied on the course. This can be used as a checklist in your preparation.

The Examination Paper

The more you understand the nature of the tasks to be completed in the examination hall the better chance you have of properly preparing yourself for the event. In most cases you are likely to be studying courses or topics which have run for some years. Usually past papers are available in the library. Listed below are a few issues which can be helpful in your preparation:

→ **Length of the examination**: this will help you in planning your time during the examination.

→ **The style of the examination:** is the examination in the form of a case study? Are the questions asking for an essay-style response, or are they framed in multi-section short answer responses? Are questions general or applied to particular situations? Are subjects discrete or do questions interrelate topics?

→ **Tasks to be completed:** how many questions are you required to answer in the time? Are all questions equally weighted? What choice do you have on the paper? Is the paper split into parts, requiring you to answer questions from each part?

→ **What is the range of topics covered on the paper?** Do you need to know all the topics from the course? Does the degree of choice give you the opportunity for selective revision? Do some topics come up regularly? Are there some current issues and debates likely to come up in the paper?

→ **What do the questions require of you?** Some questions, particularly in the early stages of a course, may be designed to check your knowledge and understanding of a topic. It is more usual, however, for the questions to require you to apply your knowledge; or to evaluate concepts and theories (see the list of examples of essay questions provided in Step 9).

Whilst the above are some general hints, each examination paper is likely to have its own style. You would be well advised to discuss the examination with your subject tutor. Check what the examiner expects in the style of answers. Is there a change in the examining team, or format of the paper? This process will be particularly important in new courses or topics where there is no backlog of past papers on which to rely.

Revision

Each year examination problems occur because students fail to prepare themselves properly for the examination. Two distinct types are detectable:

> **The over-anxious student who spends too much of the revision period in unselective reading and is thereby overwhelmed by the topic.**
>
> **The under-anxious student who leaves revision to the last minute and is thereby unprepared for the examination.**

Here are some suggestions to make your revision effective:

Planning: it is a good idea to plan for the examinations which you will have to sit by making a time plan showing the time and periods you will spend on the revision for each paper.

Make sure you give particular focus to your weaker subjects. It is a natural tendency to avoid the topics which you find most difficult.

Be realistic in your planning. Give yourself breaks. Allow time to relax, etc. Short but frequent revision is probably more effective than long intensive bursts. Time-management theory suggests that setting yourself realistic targets which you work towards is most useful.

Remember: plans need to be flexible, and you need to allow for things to go wrong. Build some spare capacity into the plan.

How to revise

Different subjects and different individuals may approach the revision process in different ways, however there are a few key principles which may be helpful.

Memory is the prevention of forgetting: your revision strategies need to adopt techniques which will stop you from forgetting what you know.

→ Make the topic interesting.

→ Use both sides of the brain by using colour, shape and diagrams in note-making.

→ Mnemonics may help. These are easily remembered phrases which trigger information which you may need to recall; Richard Of York Gave Battle In Vain is a well-known example used by those wishing to remember the colours of the rainbow.

Repeated revision and review are essential. Keyword notes and spray diagrams can be very helpful. These can help you to quickly review your notes.

The Examination

Each year students appear to make very similar errors in the way that they approach the examination process. Here are a few of the most common.

Running out of time: a failure to allow enough time to attempt all questions is a very common mistake. Often this is caused by spending too much time on the earlier questions. Generally, it is better to attempt all questions, rather than hope to maximize your marks on the first questions.

Failure to answer the question: under the stress of the examination, it is very easy to misread the question and give the wrong answer. In some cases a student regurgitates what he/she knows on the topic, but does not apply it to the subject or specific focus required.

Lack of preparation: some students experience examination difficulties because they just fail to prepare themselves properly for the examination. Frequently, the problem is based on a lack of understanding of what will be expected of them and they fail to plan the examination properly.

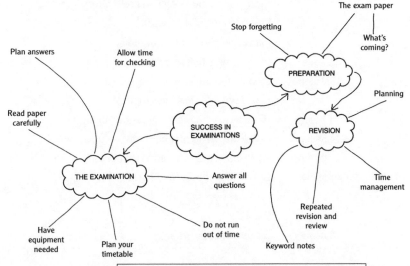

Figure 11.1 A Spray Diagram for Examination Success

A Step-by-Step Guide

Prior to the examination

Plan your time in the exam: you should enter the examination with a well-defined plan of how you will spend your time. Allow time to read the examination paper, and to both plan and check your answers. Many students mistakenly think that they must spend the whole of the examination period writing down everything they know. Examiners will be more impressed with well-focused answers.

Avoid last minute revision: this is rarely effective. It is better to keep your mind clear and free from anxiety.

Make sure you are clear about where and when the examination will take place: Arrive in good time and try to avoid any situation which will distract you or make you anxious.

Table 11.1 Example of Examination Time Plan For a Three Hour, Equally Weighted, Three Question Exam

9.00 a.m.	Examination commences
	Read examination paper and select questions
	Plan answer to first question
	Plan answer to second question
9.20 a.m.	Write answer to first question (45 min)
10.05 a.m.	Stop writing first answer
	Plan answer to third question
10.10 a.m.	Write answer to second question (45 min)
10.55 a.m.	Check answer to first question
11.00 a.m.	Write answer to third question (45 min)
11.45 a.m.	Check answer to second question
11.50 a.m.	Check answer to third question
11.55 a.m.	Final check
12 noon	Examination finishes

Make sure you have all the equipment you need: spare pens, pencils, calculators (if allowed), rulers, etc. You will need a working watch so you can track your time during the examination.

The time plan shown in Table 11.1 is based on a 3-hour traditional examination requiring three essay-style answers. Note how there is time allowed for planning and for checking answers, and frequent changes of activity.

In the examination

> **MAKE SURE YOU FILL IN THE FRONT SHEET OF THE EXAMINATION BOOK ACCURATELY**

→ **Carefully read the examination paper**: choose the questions and how you will answer them. If given the choice, start with your strongest answer. Think about the question and what it is asking of you.

→ **Before you start to write, plan your answer**: it is a good idea to plan the first couple of questions before you start to answer the first question. Spray diagrams are useful and you can add to them as you go through the exam.

→ **Write the first answer**: where appropriate use references to support your discussion. Keep within the time target which you have set. Allow plenty of room on the paper. Try to make it easy for the examiner to see what you know. Do not write in the examination book margins.

→ **Plan the third question before you start the second**: this method of planning a question in advance helps you to answer and plan questions more effectively. Often the planning or writing of one answer will help with the planning and writing of another.

→ **Write the answer to the second question:** if ideas come to you relating to the other questions add them to your notes.

→ **Check your answer to the first question**: remove spelling mistakes, etc., and add any additional information which has come to you.

→ **Try to work closely to your timetable**: with a proper plan you should be able to make a good attempt at all questions.

Revision and Review

✓ Effective examination preparation starts at the beginning of the course or module.

✓ Try to prevent forgetting by constant revision and review.

✓ Make sure you know the form of the examination and type of questions you will be asked.

✓ Build your revision towards the examination.

✓ Draw up your examination timetable.

✓ In the examination work to your timetable.

The Dissertation

In this step you will consider:

✓ *The benefits of the dissertation exercise*

✓ *The dissertation process*

✓ *Selecting the topic and research question*

✓ *The written document*

Introduction

The aim of this session is to introduce you to some of the topics that surround the crafting of a dissertation. It is not the authors' intention for this to be used as a substitute for reading and referring to specific books dedicated to the subject.

Most undergraduate and postgraduate students will, in the course of their studies, be required to produce a dissertation or project. This piece of work will depend entirely upon the student's individual research and learning abilities, as well as reflecting the degree of time and effort invested in this process. In most instances it will represent the most profound and extensive piece of work that the student will have yet attempted. The dissertation is a test of the student's ability to plan, manage, carry out and present the outcomes of a major piece of research. Whilst very few students 'break new ground', they may become involved in the investigation of an issue from a different perspective or drawing upon new evidence.

Aims of the Dissertation

+ To enable the student to undertake a substantial piece of independent work in an area of interest that is relevant to the focus of their degree course;

+ To enable the student to demonstrate a high level of independent learning and self development, in respect of planning a major assignment, collecting information from a variety of sources, applying investigatory and analytical skills, presenting meaningful outcomes and drawing conclusions;

+ To enable the student to develop a sense of commitment and personal responsibility for their own work

◆ To encourage the student to develop a sense of commitment and personal responsibility for their own work;

◆ To provide the student with a major opportunity to draw selectively and critically upon a body of knowledge, wisdom and information to produce new insights, ideas and perspectives.

(Excerpt from Nottingham Business School's Dissertation Guidelines 2000–2001)

Benefits of the Dissertation

→ It is good for personal development and learning. During the process of 'doing the dissertation' the student develops transferable skills, for instance, how they manage their time.

→ It demonstrates the student's ability to prospective employers; this is especially true if the dissertation has relevance to the sector the student wishes to join.

→ It shows an ability to cope with the research process. The way in which research questions are dealt with informs the reader of the student's ability to *think*.

→ It demonstrates self-management, self-motivation and problem solving skills.

→ It shows the student's intellectual, organizational and communication skills.

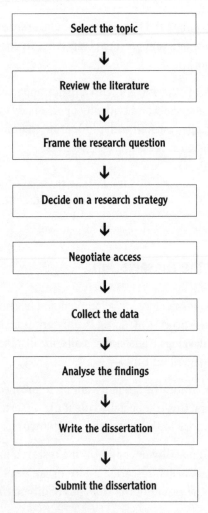

Figure 12.1 Nine Stages in the Dissertation Process

Selecting the Topic

Up until the point in the course where students are required to undertake research for their dissertations, they have been involved, largely, with answering questions that other people have set. At first, the notion of selecting the topic and the research question for a dissertation, can be daunting but there are techniques that can help generate ideas. These can be broken down into two categories: rational and creative thinking.

The rational/logical techniques

Examining your own strengths and interests: the best place to start is an area where you have developed a genuine interest, either through your academic studies or a work placement. It is worth considering any recent assignments that attracted particularly high marks, as it is likely these will be topics that are of interest.

Looking at past dissertations: most university libraries house past projects. Browsing through the titles of these may generate a topic idea.

Searching the literature: at this point, books will probably be the least likely source of ideas concerning current issues and debates. More useful will be any recent trade, or professional magazines, which should give a wealth of ideas on which to build. Another source of topics are academic review articles and journals, these often contain recommendations for further work within specific disciplines.

Discussion: often having a chat with friends, or practitioners, will stimulate debate and discussion that lead to a topic area. It is always advisable to talk through any ideas with the dissertation tutor, or supervisor. They are experienced in both supervising and marking dissertations and will be able to steer you clear of potential problem areas.

Having considered some rational/logical techniques for helping to find a dissertation topic, we will now look at more creative methods. In the earlier session on learning styles we discussed the left- and right-side of the brain functions and discovered that creative techniques will not suit everyone.

Creative techniques

Keeping a notebook of ideas: sometimes ideas come at the most unexpected times, this is the result of the sub-conscious working away at a persistent, or difficult problem while the brain is actively engaged in another activity, or even sleeping. If these ideas are not recorded they can be lost. Some people regularly keep a notebook by the side of their beds to record ideas that they have whilst they sleep.

Relevance trees: this concept is similar to that of mind mapping. The idea is to start with one idea, usually a broad concept, from which you generate further more specific topics. In other words you work back from the subjects that most interest you. Several of these sub-topics can be combined to provide a research idea.

Brain storming: this technique is usually associated with problem solving within a business or management environment, but can be adopted to generate research ideas. This activity is conducted amongst a group of people. The first stage is to ask participants for *any* ideas, however vague, or irrelevant they may seem. No contribution should be evaluated, or criticized – at this stage *every* suggestion should carry equal weight. As many suggestions as possible should be encouraged. These ideas are then all written down on a board, after that they are considered, explored and evaluated by the group. Often the combination of several of these will result in a relevant and interesting area for research.

This is not meant to be an exhaustive list of techniques, rather some that the authors have successfully employed in the past to stimulate areas for research.

Ultimately the topic should:

→ Have a clear focus: it should be possible to define clearly and concisely what the dissertation will seek to achieve. This is an area where a lot of students fall down; they often focus on too broad an area and address too many issues.

→ Be relevant to the degree, or course, you are undertaking.

→ Be realistic and manageable: it should be possible to complete a first degree dissertation within an average of about eight hours' work each week over a six month period.

→ Represent a new, different, or more up-to-date line of enquiry.

→ Be capable of being investigated; you will have access to primary data.

→ Be interesting enough that it will sustain your interest over a six to nine month period.

Reviewing the Literature

Most students have some vague notion that they have to 'do a literature review' but few understand the reason *why* they need to undertake this task. The most important reason is that to understand the topic fully you need to engage in reading around the subject. This provides an insight into the issues to be investigated. This not only includes reading books, but also journals, newspapers, conference papers and theses and, increasingly, the use of Information Technology. Because of the advance of Information Technology researchers now have access to a far wider range and source of information than they have had in the past. Use should be made of various electronic indexes, CD Roms and the Internet.

Another reason for looking at the literature is that you can see what studies have been carried out before and what strategies previous researchers have used. Furthermore a review might identify where there is a gap in knowledge surrounding the topic. What follows are, what might be called, 'rules of engagement':

→ Use as up-to-date material as possible. Unless they are classic theories, don't discuss outdated materials.

→ Critically evaluate the material that you review.

→ Use as wide a variety of sources as is practicable, where appropriate deal with a range of theories and perspectives, this will demonstrate thoroughness.

→ Identify and discuss key turning points and studies to do with the topic.

→ Remember to discuss and analyse concepts, not just produce a list of authors and titles. Advice has been given in Step 9 *Essays and Reports* concerning sequencing written material.

Framing the research question

It is the authors' belief that the selection of the topic is the single most important aspect of researching for and writing of a dissertation. Much of this area has already been covered in Step 7 *Gathering Information*. Having decided upon a topic, further issues have to be addressed, which will be examined in this section.

The first thing to consider is the *aims* of the research. Often students are over-ambitious with their aims and have to be encouraged to focus down. Here is an example of an original research proposal. *'The research will examine the relationship between training and labour turnover within the hotel industry'*. After consulting with their tutor the student changed their title to: *'The research will examine the relationship between training and labour turnover within two hotels in Leeds'*. What is the researcher (please note that the student will be referred to as the researcher from now on, because that is exactly what they will become) trying to achieve? By answering this they will begin to think about what the research might show. This is an important stage as it leads on nicely to stating some *objectives*. These need to be clearly articulated and be measurable, because one of the criteria by which the success of the dissertation will be judged is how well conclusions were drawn from the data collected. This is far easier to demonstrate if the objectives have been clearly stated at the beginning of the process.

Deciding on a research approach

Most authors, when addressing this topic tend to dedicate much time and considerable space to the philosophies that under-pin any good research project. It is not the intention of the authors to address this area at all (there are already many excellent books on this subject), but rather to concentrate on more practical issues. Having decided upon a topic and framed the research question, the next stage is to consider *what* information you are looking for and *how* you intend to find it. The research design forms the framework of the entire research process detailing the most suitable methods of investi-gation, nature of research instruments, sampling plans and types of qualitative and quantitative data. Quantitative information is numerical and statistical, usually measured on a scale. The findings can be manipulated by statistical techniques. Qualitative information is non-numerical, relating to characteristics or people's opinions.

In the process of answering the two questions, *what* informa-tion you are looking for and *how* you intend to find it, other issues will emerge, for example:

♦ *What research methods will be employed?*

♦ *What will my sample size be?*

♦ *Where will I draw my sample from?*

♦ *How will I get access?*

♦ *Are there any ethical issues to consider?*

Underpinning the answers to these questions consideration must be given to the notions of *validity* and *reliability*, that is the credibility of the research findings. Simply put, reliability concerns itself with the dependability of the data collected. A reliable measure is one, which gives the same or very similar, results if another researcher replicates the original research, using the same individuals and the same research design under the same conditions. Reliability describes consistency.

Validity is about whether the method of data collection is sound or true, in that it is thought to measure what it sets out to measure. For example, if social survey observations are said to be valid, then they are considered to be a true reflection of the phenomenon being examined in the population being studied. Any research topic must satisfy the conditions of both reliability and validity to be considered 'sound'.

There are many diverse methods of information gathering, all have pros and cons. Some of these methods were considered in Step 7 *Gathering Information*. The choice of method depends upon several factors: access, time available, complexity of the task and other variables. Information, or data, falls into two categories, primary and secondary. In the simplest terms: primary research consists of original data collected for the specific purpose at hand; secondary data are concerned with information that already exists. Within these two groups are two distinct methods of research, those of qualitative and quantitative research methods.

Quantitative research is concerned with any method that results in the data being presented in numerical form, often appearing as graphs and pie charts. Students have a tendency towards such methods, as they feel 'safe' with such graphs as it gives them a sense of 'authority'. The types of data collection within this category would include: questionnaires, interviews and observation.

Qualitative research is concerned with meanings and the way people understand things and a concern with patterns of behaviour. Some examples of methods that are qualitative are: interviews, participant observation and field notes and a research questionnaire.

A brief synopsis of the relative strengths and weaknesses are found below

Qualitative research

Strengths	Weaknesses
✦ The data and analysis are 'grounded'	✦ The data may be less representative
✦ There is richness and detail to the data	✦ Interpretation might be subjective and bound up with the 'self' of the researcher
✦ There is a tolerance of ambiguity and contradiction	✦ There is a possibility of decontextualizing the meaning
✦ There is the prospect of alternative explanations	✦ There is a danger of oversimplifying the explanation

Quantitative research

Strengths	Weaknesses
✦ Is seen as objective	✦ It is possible to use secondary data that were not collected for the research purpose and misuse it
✦ Data are easily analysed and manipulated	
✦ Can deal with large numbers, which are representative and increases population validity	✦ It is possible to analyse and adversely manipulate the interpretation of results
✦ The process of data collection is distinct from the analysis	✦ There is no room for ambiguity in the questions

Some of the more common research methods were covered in Step 7 *'Gathering Information'*. Whichever method is used it is useful to employ the content analysis set out in the box below before deciding upon a question.

Question content

For each question ask:

- ◆ Is the question necessary?

- ◆ Will the question elicit the required data?

- ◆ Does the respondent understand the question?

- ◆ Does the respondent have the necessary information to answer the question?

- ◆ Is the respondent willing, or able, to answer the questions?

Question phrasing

For each question avoid:

- ◆ Complex phrases and long words

- ◆ Long and rambling questions

- ◆ Ambiguous and vague wording

- ◆ Biased words and leading or loaded questions?

- ◆ Negative questions

- ◆ Asking two questions in one

- ◆ Asking personal questions

Negotiating access

Once they have identified a topic and started to read around
the subject, most researchers want to go out and get on with
what they perceive is the most enjoyable part of the dissertation;
the actual live research. Often with little thought about gaining
access, this is an area that should be given careful consideration.

Access is often problematic, and there can be several reasons
for this. The first is the most widely encountered. With increasing
numbers of students entering higher education, some companies
are saturated with requests from students wishing to conduct
research within their organizations. They simply do not have the
resources to engage in additional, voluntary activities due to the
resourcing implications. The company may have some doubt as to
the researcher's abilities and competence. What is their credibility?
The final problem is that sometimes the subject area is too sensitive,
and the company is concerned about the confidentiality of any
dissertation a university student might present. After all no
company wants to be shown in a negative way. An example of this
is that one of our students wanted to engage in research that looked
at the efficacy and ethics of marketing carbonated alcoholic drinks
to teenagers. They seemed surprised that they could not get an
interview with one of the large breweries that sold such beverages.

There are strategies that can help the researcher to gain access.
Allow sufficient *time*. If the researcher is trying to access a large
organization, it may take several attempts and several weeks to
succeed. An exploratory telephone call is a good idea to establish
just who needs to be contacted. An e-mail request should also be
considered. A clear statement is required as to what precisely is
required from that person. This is an ideal opportunity to establish
credibility and let that person know what they might expect in
return for allowing access.

If relevant, the researcher might consider their *work placement*. To see if there is any topic that could be researched there.
Providing that it was a positive experience, that should satisfy the

condition of establishing credibility and contacts should have already been made. Much in the same vein, if the researcher has friends or relatives working in an establishment of interest, that might provide access.

The compilation of an *introductory letter* should be given serious consideration. This should include a brief outline of the research and the precise nature of the request. If possible the researcher should emphasize that their involvement will cause minimal disruption to the day-to-day running of the operation. If relevant, they should state that complete anonymity and confidentiality will be guaranteed. They should include a stamped self-addressed envelope and give the person whose permission they want as many ways of contacting them as possible – telephone, fax and, increasingly, e-mail address. An example of such a letter can be found in Figure 12.2.

It can also be of benefit to offer a copy of the report of your findings to the participating organization. They will be giving you access and their staff time, in exchange for a consultancy style report. It is always advisable to tailor a specific report for the company rather that just give them a copy of your finished dissertation, as the styles may be very different. Once the letter is sent out it is a good idea to write down the detail of exactly what it is you want from that organization and how you intend to collect that information, should you gain access. Keep this list by the telephone, because if the company does 'phone you, you will be able to sound confident, competent and in control; it might just be a composed telephone manner that impresses them enough to give you access.

To summarize:

→ Leave plenty of time to gain access.

→ Think about using an establishment, or an organization where the researcher has friends, or family working as a place to research.

Home Address:-
e-mail
Telephone/Fax No

22nd August 2000

Their Address

Dear Doctor ***.

Research into General Practice

I am currently researching into general practice for my M.Phil. and I have spoken to a colleague of mine about the possibility of meeting you to discuss the above. I am hoping to conduct four in-depth case studies, which will involve several visits to the participating practices over a period of some weeks. Much of the research will involve me just sitting and watching how the 'normal day' proceeds and will not interfere with anyone's workload. I would also like to conduct a few interviews (of about one hour in duration) with the senior partner and the practice manager.

Some of the information that I am hoping to obtain will be of a confidential nature, firstly this information will only be published preserving complete anonymity (i.e. practice X had such and such a ratio) and only with the express permission of the practice. The second point is that the practice can determine which figures I will have access to. I have scheduled overleaf an example of the type of information I am aiming to obtain and how I hope to achieve this.

One of the benefits from the practice's perspective is that I will produce a report for them that will include some degree of audit that may well be useful for inclusion in the practice report.

I am currently conducting a pilot study in Derbyshire. The senior partner there has said that he would be very willing to give me a reference emphasizing that my presence at the practice did not disrupt the working day and also to attest to my integrity.

I do hope that you feel able to allow me to use your practice as a case study. If there is anything else that you would like to know, I'd be only too happy to come over and talk to you about it.

Yours sincerely

Figure 12.2 An Introductory Letter

- Even if the initial contact has been by telephone, always follow this up with an introductory letter.

- Be clear and precise about what exactly you want the organization to provide.

- Increase credibility by showing clarity of thought when articulating the purpose of the research.

- Try to allay any concerns the organization may have about the amount of disruption that might be caused.

Writing the Dissertation

Much of the techniques for academic writing have been covered in Step 9, with particular emphasis on grammar and spelling. We will now look at referencing and the presentation of the dissertation. As most students have difficulties with referencing, we shall look at this topic in more detail.

Referencing
Why reference?
Essentially there are two reasons for referencing. Firstly it allows the writer to define clearly what is their own work and what is the work of another author. That way the person marking a piece of work can identify original pieces of writing from that of others. It also gives credit to the original authors, common courtesy demands that their efforts are acknowledged. To attempt to take the credit for someone else's work and present it as your own is known as 'plagiarism' (from the French for kidnap *Plagiare*. This is seen as a very serious offence, sometimes resulting in a student being expelled from their course. For this reason it is *strongly recommended* that when notes are made from various readings,

details are carefully recorded of: the author; name of book; year of publication; name of publishers, and where appropriate the page number (if a direct word for word copy is made from the author).

The second reason for referencing is that it enables the reader to go to the original text. They might be very interested in a specific topic within the writing and wish to research it further.

Where do you reference?

There are two places where references are made, firstly within the text of what is written and also at the end within a section called 'references' or 'Bibliography'. To allow for consistency it is necessary to use a method of referencing. This also allows the reader to evaluate the depth of the study. The Harvard referencing system is a widely accepted method of referencing for academic dissertations.

How do you reference?

Within the text

If use is being made of someone else's idea, but not directly quoting from their book, or article it would look like this:

Northouse (2000) points out that contingency theory considers the situation is as important as the leader's style in determining managerial effectiveness.

However if you are quoting directly from an author's text you usually indent the passage, give it two spaces before and after and treat it like this:

'Contingency theory represents a shift in leadership research from focusing only on the leader, to looking at the leader in conjunction with the situation in which the leader works' (P. Northouse, 2000: 86).

Here we have shown that we are using the author's own words and we have identified not only the year of publication but the page as being page 86. If someone reading this wishes to look more fully at the context in which the quote is made they can easily find the exact passage.

Within the text *all* sources of information are treated in this way, these might be from: books; journal articles; magazines; newspapers, or even the internet.

In the Bibliography

The list is alphabetical, according to author's surnames and the years of publication. If an author has published more than one article or book in a year then the order is designated by the use of a lower case letter in alphabetical order, after the year of publication, thus 1999(a).

Within the bibliography specific sources of information are dealt with slightly differently. The conventions for these and examples are listed below; this is followed by combining the examples and showing them as they should appear in the bibliography.

For a book the sequence of entry is thus:

1. Surname and initial of author.
2. Date of publication in brackets.
3. Title of book emphasized (either by underlining or in italics).
4. Publisher.
5. Place of publication.

For example:

Northouse, P. G. (2000) *Leadership, Theory and Practice*, Sage, London.

For an essay or chapter from an edited book:

1. Surname and initial of author.
2. Date of publication in brackets.
3. Title of chapter underlined.
4. In/from editor's name(s) followed by (ed.) or (eds).
5. Title of the book emphasized.
6. Place of publication and publisher.
7. Page numbers of the whole chapter.

For example:

Greenfield, S. and Nayak, A. (1996) <u>A management role for the general practitioner?</u>, In Leopold, J., Glover, I. and Hughes, M. (eds) *Beyond Reason? The National Health Service and the Limits of Management*, Ashgate Publishing, Aldershot, pp. 59–80.

For journal entries:

1. Surname and initial of author.
2. Date of publication in brackets.
3. Title of article underlined.
4. Title of journal emphasized.
5. Publication details – volume (a volume normally relates to a year) and number (usually relates to an issue).
6. Page numbers of the whole article.

For example:

Lashley, C. (1999) <u>Employee empowerment in services: a framework for analysis</u>, *Personnel Review*, Vol. 28, No. 3, pp 169–191.

For Internet entries:

1. Surname and initial of author.
2. Title of article emphasized.
3. To indicate that it is an Internet entry put in brackets (online).
4. The URL (Universal Resource Locator) address.
5. The date that you accessed the page in brackets.

For example:

Brown, S. (1999) *Service Quality and Customer Satisfaction Survey* (online).URL:http://www.hweb.co.uk/ simonbrown>. (Accessed 12 April 1999.)

If we now put all these examples together we will see what the contents of a (very small) bibliography might look like.

Bibliography

Brown, S. (1999) *Service Quality and Customer Satisfaction Survey* (online).URL:http://www.hweb.co.uk/ simonbrown>. (Accessed 12 April 1999.)

Greenfield, S. and Nayak, A. (1996) A management role for the general practitioner? In Leopold, J., Glover, I. and Hughes, M. (eds) *Beyond Reason? The National Health Service and the Limits of Management*, Ashgate Publishing, Aldershot, pp. 59–80.

Lashley, C. (1999) Employee empowerment in services: a framework for analysis, *Personnel review*, Vol. 28, No. 3, pp. 169–191.

Northouse, P. G. (2000) *Leadership, Theory and Practice*, Sage, London.

Presentation of the dissertation

It is important to comply to the university regulations; however, most universities base their standards on British Standard BS 4821, a synopsis of which is shown in Figure 12.3.

Relationship with the Supervisor

This relationship is crucial. Whilst each tutor, or supervisor, will supervise using their individual and preferred method, it *is* possible to give general advice. The first is to impress them with enthusiasm for the task, demonstrate this by turning up for all appointments, for instance. Tutors are only human and they will tend to respond more positively to students who can show that they really are trying their best. If a time scale is agreed upon to complete a specific task, then it must be achieved, or in extenuating circumstances a revised and realistic completion time needs to be communicated to the tutor in good time. If the tutor gives advice that you don't agree with then discuss this point and articulate your misgivings. An area where the tutor is likely to be of great help is in pointing you in the right direction to find information; they may have knowledge of a specific publication, for instance.

It has to be remembered here that this is *your* piece of work not the supervisor's and you should not expect *too* much input from them. Often the tutor will counter a question with another question and seldom give concrete solutions.

Time Management

As this is likely to be the single most important piece of academic work that the researcher will have attempted to date, and span a longer time period than any other project, managing time is essential. Once a topic has been selected, the researcher needs to list and prioritize all the tasks ahead and attempt to put a time-scale to each of those tasks. There is a need to be *realistic* about this, when scheduling the tasks the student has to take into account other essays, reports and presentations that will also make demands on time. Holidays must not be forgotten, particularly Christmas and the New Year. Potential respondents might be too busy during this period and the student might have social events planned.

Length	10,000–15,000 words
Copies	2 + copies to be submitted to the university
Main Elements	**(indicative)**
	1. Title Page
	2. Abstract
Overview	3. List of Contents
Technicalities	4. List of illustrations and tables
	5. Acknowledgements
	6. Definitions and/or abbreviations
	7. Main body of the text
	Introduction and aims of the research
Argument	Review of the literature
Knowledge	Methodology and data-collection
	techniques
Research	Results
	Discussion
	Conclusion/recommendations (including
	strengths and weaknesses of research
	and further research to be done)
	8. Appendices (optional)
Literature	9. Glossary (optional)
Search	10. Bibliography of items cited in the text
	11. Bibliography of items read but not cited in
	the text
Title Page	Full title, including subtitle
	Your full name
	Qualification for which the dissertation is being
	submitted
	Name of organization to which the dissertation
	is being submitted
	Relevant department, or faculty
	Month and year of submission

Layout and Presentation	A4 paper $70g/m^2$–$100g/m^2$ white
	Word processed, or printed using clear type face (not italic, or fancy)
	Twelve point for main text
	Double spacing of lines/quotes and footnotes single space
	Margins left hand = 30mm, right hand = 20mm
	Paragraphs flush left
	Quotes longer than five lines indent by five characters
	Number all pages – normally centred bottom of page
	Chapters to start on new page.

Figure 12.3 Synopsis of British Standard BS 4821

One of the best tools to enable this is the use of a *Gannt chart*. A Gannt chart lists the items to do, along with associated time frames, and resources with start and end dates. It is the tactical roadmap to help execute the project. Effectively it is a step-by-step listing of everything that is planned to do. The actual chart shows a visual graph illustrating the correlation and possible overlap between activities. One of the advantages of using such a chart is that it is visual, the researcher can see at a glance where he/she should be and what should have been done by a specific time. It is a helpful tool to get back 'on track' should there be any 'slippage'. An example is shown in Figure 12.4, although it is more usual for the chart to be in landscape, rather than portrait.

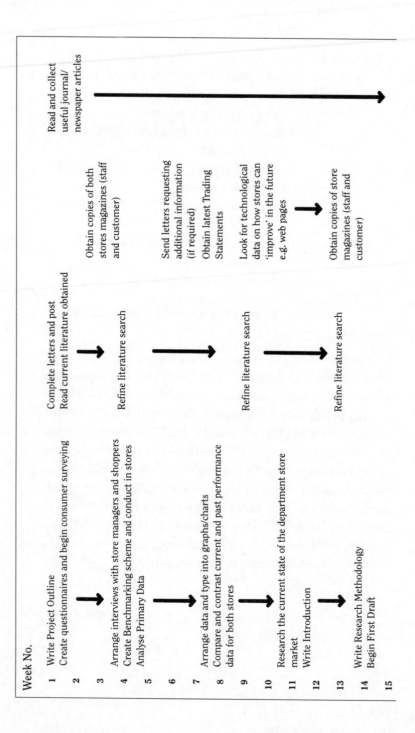

Week No.

1 Write Project Outline
2 Create questionnaires and begin consumer surveying

Complete letters and post
Read current literature obtained

Read and collect useful journal/ newspaper articles

3 Arrange interviews with store managers and shoppers
4 Create Benchmarking scheme and conduct in stores
5 Analyse Primary Data

Refine literature search

Obtain copies of both stores magazines (staff and customer)

6
7 Arrange data and type into graphs/charts
8 Compare and contrast current and past performance data for both stores

Refine literature search

Send letters requesting additional information (if required)
Obtain latest Trading Statements
Look for technological data on how stores can 'improve' in the future e.g. web pages

9
10 Research the current state of the department store market
11
12 Write Introduction

Refine literature search

Obtain copies of store magazines (staff and customer)

13
14 Write Research Methodology
15 Begin First Draft

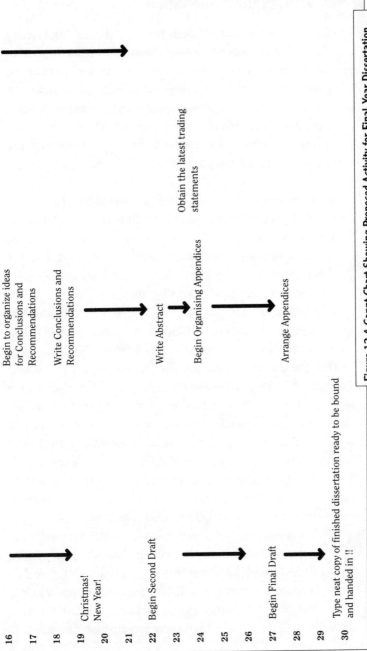

Figure 12.4 Gannt Chart Showing Proposed Activity for Final Year Dissertation

Writing the Dissertation

The next piece of advice might seem strange, but it really helps if the researcher chooses the right location for writing the dissertation. Once somewhere has been found where the researcher is comfortable, it might be at home, a particular spot in a classroom, or in the library, the researcher's mind will quickly associate that place with dissertation activity. The sub-conscious will come into play and it will be surprising how quickly the researcher will be able to get into the right mind set for creative writing.

It is very important to get writing as soon as possible. At that stage it really doesn't matter what the quality of the output is, but it is vital to get something down on paper or the screen. What has been written can be edited later. For example this section of the chapter was originally written as an imaginary conversation with a student during a dissertation supervision session. It was full of 'you's and your's'. The last sentence of the last paragraph originally read: '*Your sub-conscious will kick in and you'll be real surprised how quick you'll be able to get into gear and the creative juices will flow*'. Clearly here some of the rules of grammar, discussed earlier, were being broken, we shouldn't write as we speak. However using this device of writing up an imaginary conversation, got enough of the salient points down on paper, to be edited later. It is so important to write *something*, the longer anyone stares at a blank sheet of paper, or a blank screen, the harder it is to start. Many a student has fallen into the trap of being too easily distracted and wasted much time playing solitaire, or mine sweeper on the computer instead of writing!

It depends how disciplined and motivated the researcher is, but some students benefit from false horizons. That is bringing deadlines forward by two or three weeks, such a strategy does have benefits. The first is that it allows some contingency time, if the student is unfortunate enough to have a personal problem, or are off sick for a while, then there is a cushion that will take care of that and they will not be under so much pressure. The second benefit is that if they do finish the project a couple of weeks ahead of their real schedule they have that time to refine the project. Often it is possible to improve the final dissertation enough to raise it a whole classification just by thoroughly proof reading it. It is a good idea to let someone else read what is thought to be the final draft, often a person reading the dissertation for the first time will spot things that have been missed, such as poor grammar, or ambiguity.

Common Problem Areas Encountered by Students

Time management

◆ Students don't start early enough

◆ Don't leave enough time to write it up

Not enough reading round the subject

Contact with Tutor is poor

Lack of focus

◆ Students underestimate the sheer weight of the work

Access

◆ This needs to be negotiated and sorted out as early as possible

Overuse of questionnaires

◆ Often students are overconfident about the return rate

Revision and Review

✓ The benefits of undergoing the dissertation process are many and varied.

✓ The choice of topic is crucial, if interest is to be sustained in the dissertation for several months.

✓ The relationship with your tutor is vital and should be managed.

✓ Time-management techniques can make effective use of a scarce resource . . . time.

✓ Produce and use a Gannt chart.

✓ It is vital to attribute sources throughout the dissertation. It is recommended that the 'Harvard' system is used.

✓ Spelling and grammar should be thoroughly checked before the final copy of the dissertation is submitted.

PART C

Study Competence

Achieving Study Competence

Introduction

This book has attempted to provide guidance and advice on a range of issues, which will improve the effectiveness of your efforts as a student. A distinguishing feature of the text, however, is that it does not stop at giving advice and guidance.

Part A outlined three key assumptions about study, learning and performance. Firstly you can be more effective in the way you study and approach assessment. Secondly you will gain most by active involvement in your study skill development – you should complete the exercises outlined in this book. Thirdly an ongoing commitment to improve the standard of your work will stem from the use of performance criteria.

This part outlines the activities, which make up effective study performance criteria required for successful study activities. It also suggests a means by which you can actively use these performance criteria to both improve your efforts and demonstrate that you have achieved competent performance.

Defining Competence

Competence-based assessment is widely used in programmes that lead to the award of National Vocational Qualifications (NVQs) and General National Vocational Qualifications (GNVQs). Essentially competence is concerned with performance of work-based tasks. In these work-based programmes, competence is the ability to perform activities within an occupation. Whilst the activities outlined here are not linked to an occupation, these concepts provide a useful model for you to apply in your study activities. The following section employs a number of terms from this wider approach to the development of competence and these terms are identified and defined below.

Competence: you will be considered to be competent in your study performance when you are able to perform all study activities competently.

Key roles: these are the broadest descriptions of activities that make up study performance, in this case, study preparation, study, and assessment of study.

Units: these describe the activities, which make up competent study performance; for example, reading, note making, and examinations.

Elements: describe the things, which you should be able to do – they are indications of behaviour, actions or outcomes.

Performance criteria: describe what competent performance looks like. They indicate what is required for the successful achievement of the element.

To achieve competence in study activities, it is necessary, therefore, to undertake the full range of study activities in a way which demonstrates competence. To demonstrate competence, study performance should match the performance criteria, which follow.

Demonstrating Competence

This text is designed to be used flexibly. It was suggested in Part A that there were at least three possible ways of working:

→ on your own

→ in pairs or small groups with other students

→ developing study skills through the course

In each case it is necessary to demonstrate competent study behaviour. This text aims to assist you to be more effective in your study activities by highlighting the criteria through which competent performance can be demonstrated.

The Storyboard Technique

The Storyboard Technique is a device that is widely used in the assessment of effective work-based performance. It can also be useful in demonstrating competent study performance. To achieve this you produce a portfolio, which covers all the units of competence and their supporting elements and shows how your study activities meet all the appropriate performance criteria.

You start by selecting a unit and writing a story, or series of stories, which describe what you did in that activity. Each story is written in the first person, describes what you did, and demonstrates how your behaviour meets the performance criteria associated with that activity. Each story is supported by evidence.

NOTE: it is not always possible to come up with a 'story' which allows you to demonstrate all performance criteria. This is why you may need to write more than one story. It is important, however, that all the storyboards (study situations which you describe) for a particular unit do cover, with evidence, all the performance criteria for the unit.

Evidence

The evidence, which you use to support your claim for competent performance, may include a wide range of materials, which you produce for normal study and assessment activities. Here are just a few suggestions:

→ notes made during research for an essay

→ materials gathered from teaching situations

→ notes made in preparation for an exam

→ essays or reports which have been assessed

→ testimony from other students with whom you have worked

→ action plans and timetables

Verification

Once you have completed a unit, you give the unit storyboards and supporting evidence to a 'significant other' (friend, fellow student or tutor) for verification. The verification process checks that your claims to meet the performance criteria have been supported by evidence. A second opinion is crucial here.

Once this has been agreed and verified, have the appropriate unit 'signed off' on the header sheet at the end of Part C. Continue to work through the units in this way until you have completed all units.

Study Skills:
A Competence Approach

Study Competences

Key Role: Study Preparation

Step 1 Adopting a learning style

Element 1.1 Calculating learning style

Performance criteria
1. Identifies own preferred learning style
2. Points out advantages of this style
3. Points out the disadvantages of this style
4. Is aware of benefits of other styles
5. Is aware of weaknesses of other styles

Element 1.2 Maintaining an effective learning style

Performance criteria
1. Takes action to amend own style
2. Actively considers learning style in study activities

Step 2 The process of learning

Element 2.1 Understanding the learning process

Performance criteria
1. Considers own left and right side brain functions
2. Produces mnemonics to aid recall
3. Applies time-management techniques to account for optimal recall
4. Adopts a task schedule to reduce anxiety

Element 2.2 Applying the learning skills

Performance criteria
1. Applies mnemonics to aid memory
2. Frequently reviews and revises notes
3. Practises tasks

Step 3 Organizing study

Element 3.1 Planning study activities

Performance criteria
1. Calculates the amount of time to be spent in support of studies
2. Produces a study timetable
3. Applies time-management techniques in planning study
4. Produces action lists
5. Adopts an appropriate use of time from own learning needs
6. Identifies resources needed for study tasks

Element 3.2 Organizing study activities

Performance criteria
1. Adopts a systematic approach to study
2. Uses plans and action lists in study activities
3. Uses both sides of the brain in study activities
4. Regularly changes activity in study tasks
5. Maintains memory through regular revision and review of notes and other materials

Key Role: Study

Step 4 Reading

Element 4.1 Selecting the reading style appropriate to the task

Performance criteria
1. Considers the purpose and study need
2. Surveys the text
3. Identifies questions to be answered
4. Reads with a purpose
5. Takes active steps to improve recall
6. Reviews information

Element 4.2 Developing reading skills

Performance criteria
1. Adopts systematic approach to improve reading skills
2. Takes steps to improve reading speed
3. Appropriate action is taken to improve vocabulary

Step 5 Note-making

Element 5.1 Adopting different note-making techniques as appropriate to different situations

Performance criteria
1. Makes notes in summary form
2. Makes outline notes
3. Makes keyword notes
4. Makes notes which use both sides of the brain
5. Applies the form of note-making which is appropriate to the study task
6. Actively reviews notes through the study period.

Step 6 Teaching and learning

Element 6.1 Selecting learning strategies for different teaching situations

Performance criteria
1. Prepares for lectures, seminars and tutorials
2. Raises questions to be addressed in learning situations
3. Plans groupwork to overcome difficulties
4. Regularly reviews work from lectures, seminars and tutorials

Element 6.2 Participating effectively in learning situations

Performance criteria
1. Actively takes part in lectures, seminars and tutorials
2. Regularly raises questions
3. Takes part in discussions where appropriate
4. Actively takes part in group situations
5. Contributes to the creation of a supportive and active learning environment

Step 7 Gathering information

Element 7.1 Adopting a systematic approach to gathering information

Performance criteria
1. Plans information needs guided by aims and objectives
2. Raises key questions to be addressed through information gathered
3. Identifies the potential sources of information available

Element 7.2 Gathering information from appropriate sources

Performance criteria
1. Gathers information with a purpose
2. Uses a variety of secondary sources of information
3. Uses a variety of primary sources of information where appropriate
4. Evaluates sources of information through consideration of validity and reliability

Element 7.3 Gathering information using a survey

Performance criteria
1. Selects an appropriate survey method
2. Selects an appropriate method for arriving at representative sample
3. Selects questions appropriate to the aims of the survey
4. Conducts the survey in an appropriate manner

Step 8 Presenting numerical data

Element 8.1 Presenting numerical data using qualitative techniques

Performance criteria
1. Uses tables and figures to support presentations
2. Tables and figures are appropriately introduced
3. Tables and figures are clearly titled and numbered
4. Categories are clearly labelled
5. Tables and figures are appropriately sourced to show the origins of the information
6. Selects the type of figure or table to best communicate the information
7. The figure or table is located close to the information in the written text

Element 8.2 Presenting numerical data using quantitative techniques

Performance criteria
1. Uses quantitative techniques when analysing data
2. Uses quantitative techniques when presenting data
3. Selects techniques appropriate to the task
4. Properly titles and labels tables, histograms and graphs
5. Basic arithmetic techniques are used in support of data analysis and presentation
6. Measures of location are used in data analysis and presentation

Key Role: Assessment of Study

Step 9 Essays and reports

Element 9.1 Writing an academic essay

Performance criteria
1. Has an appropriate structure
2. Addresses the question asked
3. Deals with a range of views and arguments
4. Demonstrates evidence of wide reading
5. Writes in an appropriate style
6. Uses appropriate references and quotations
7. Is analytical in structure
8. Is questioning in approach
9. Includes an appropriate reference/bibliography section

Element 9.2 Writing a formal report

Performance criteria
1. Has an appropriate structure
2. Uses an appropriate format with headings and sub-headings
3. Includes research methods and/or background information, where appropriate
4. Layout and presentation are to a professional standard
5. Uses quantitative and qualitative sources of information
6. Uses tables and figures to support the narrative
7. Makes appropriate conclusions and recommendations
8. Demonstrates evidence of a wide range of information sources

Step 10 Verbal presentations

Element 10.1 Making a verbal presentation

Performance criteria
1. Considers the needs of the audience
2. Meets time targets
3. Selects relevant information
4. Uses appropriate support material
5. Delivers with clarity
6. Uses appropriate eye contact and body language
7. Handles support equipment with competence
8. Answers questions with confidence

Element 10.2 Using visual aids to support verbal presentation

Performance criteria
1. Selects appropriate visual aids
2. They contain appropriate amounts of information
3. They use colour and shape where appropriate
4. Visual aids are clear and readable from all parts of the room
5. Are neat and of a professional standard

Step 11 Examinations

Element 11.1 Planning revision for examinations

Performance criteria
1. Considers the form of examination paper
2. Regularly reviews notes and information
3. Allocates sufficient time for revision
4. Plans the examination timetable
5. Selects the equipment needed for the examination

Element 11.2 Completing an examination in a systematic manner

Performance criteria
1. Plans answers to the questions
2. Uses a timetable during the exam
3. Answers all questions
4. Answers the questions as set
5. Checks answers before handing in the paper

Step 12 Dissertations

Element 12.1 Planning the dissertation

Performance criteria
1. Calculates the amount of time to be spent in support of dissertation
2. Identifies rough topic area
3. Produces a list of potential sources of information
4. Formulates the research question
5. Produces a realistic Gannt chart

Element 12.2 Organizing study activities

Performance criteria
1. Devises appropriate research mechanisms
2. Negotiates access
3. Adheres to and adapts time plan
4. Maintains contact with supervisor
5. Successfully presents dissertation on time

Study Competence Header Sheet

	Steps of competence	Not yet competent	Competent	Verifier signature
Step 1				
Step 2				
Step 3				
Step 4				
Step 5				
Step 6				
Step 7				
Step 8				
Step 9				
Step 10				
Step 11				
Step 12				

Index